MW00611847

Barbara McKay

Coming Home

Recipes and Reflections from a Life in the Spotlight

For Ann – thank you for being such a wonderful friend to me!

Enjoy and be blessed!

Barbara

SPARK Publications
Charlotte, North Carolina

Coming Home: Recipes and Reflections from a Life in the Spotlight
Barbara McKay

Designed, produced, and published by SPARK Publications
SPARKpublications.com
Charlotte, North Carolina

Front and back cover photography by Mark Hanson
Food photography by Kevin Chelko Photography

Background textures for section 1 by var_integer/Shutterstock.com,
section 2 by Love-Lava/Shutterstock.com, section 3 by Ola-la/Shutterstock.com,
and section 4 by Flaffy/Shutterstock.com. All photos edited by SPARK Publications.

Printed in the United States of America.
Hard cover, [July 2021], ISBN: 978-1-953555-13-7
Library of Congress Control Number: 2021910443

For my children,
Elizabeth and Michael

Contents

VIII The Spotlight

1 Coming Home

Fresh from the Field

4 Farm to Fork

6 Food Means Family

8 An Unexpected Hero

10 The Magic of Show Biz

14 Earning My Wings

17 New England

19 Teaching on Tobacco Road

24 Headed to Charlotte

26 Big Miracles in Tiny Packages

33 Mother Knows Best

Southern Classics

Hot Artichoke Dip ... 36
Mom's Famous Standing Rib Roast ... 37
Twice-Baked Potatoes ... 38
Garden Salad and Red Wine Vinaigrette ... 39
1-2-3-4 Cake ... 40
Chocolate Frosting for 1-2-3-4 Cake ... 41
Classic Caramel Frosting for 1-2-3-4 Cake ... 42
Pineapple Filling and Frosting for 1-2-3-4 Cake ... 43
Hot Chicken Salad ... 44
Cranberry Salad ... 45
Roasted Fresh Asparagus ... 46
Lemon Chess Pie ... 47
Sweet Potato Pie ... 49
Pumpkin Praline Pie ... 50
Tasty, Tangy Herbed Tomatoes ... 51
Asparagus New Potato Salad ... 52
Horseradish Carrots ... 53
Creamed Fresh Corn ... 54
Seasoned Corn on the Cob ... 55
Pasta Primavera ... 57
Refrigerator Vegetable Slaw ... 58
Daddy's Boiled Shrimp and Cocktail Sauce ... 59
Shrimp Creole ... 61
Baked Alaskan Halibut ... 62
Homemade Pimento Cheese ... 63
Vegetable Garden Salad ... 64
Fresh Apple Cake ... 65
Cousin's Chocolate Cake ... 66
Surprise Ham and Cheese Rolls ... 67
Homemade Chicken Noodle Soup ... 68
Chicken, Sausage, and Wild Rice Casserole ... 69
White Bean and Spinach Soup ... 71
Macaroni Beef Supper ... 72
Mississippi Corn Bread ... 73
Easy Lemonade Cake ... 74
Lobster Rolls ... 75
New England Clam Chowder ... 76
Cranberry Pecan Cornbread ... 77
The Best Brownies EVER ... 79
Goody Bars ... 80
Favorite Frosted Sugar Cookies ... 81

Screen Time

84 The Audition

86 The Adventure Begins

92 Behind the Scenes

96 New Beginnings

98 So Many Interesting People

107 Leaving WBTV

Favorite Recipes from My Daily TV Years

Taco Pie 110
Seven-Layer Mexican Dip 111
Parmesan Cheese Puffs 112
Broccoli Bread 113
Lida's Cheese Biscuits 114
Hearty Vegetable Beef Soup 115
Creamy Broccoli Soup 116
Baked Potato Soup 117
Crunchy Asian Spinach Salad 119
Curried Turkey Twist 120
Beef Enchiladas 121
Ginger Orange Beef 123
John Boy and Billy's Chili 124
Sesame Chicken Tacos 125
Dijon Sherry Chicken 126
Calabash Cove Crab Au Gratin 127
Sauteed Scallops with Pea Pods and Water Chestnuts 128
Shrimp and Creamy Grits 129
La Strada Pasta Salad 130
Seafood Fettuccine 131
Sheri Lynch's Pasta with Fresh Tomatoes 132
Baked Vidalia Onions 133
Elvis Presley Pound Cake 135
Roasted Vegetables Parmesan 136
Cheerwine Cake 137
Killer Key Lime Pie 138

Spoonfuls of Goodness

142 Moving On

143 Life without Daily TV

148 Clients Were Always Friends

151 Animal Advocacy

154 My Passion for Fashion

New Favorite Recipes

Spicy Toasted Pecans ... 162
Great Guacamole ... 163
Spicy Black Bean Soup ... 164
Favorite Onion Soup ... 165
Hot Spiced Cider ... 167
Tomato Bisque ... 168
Cornucopia Salad ... 169
Curried Rice Salad ... 170
Lemon Ginger Chicken Salad ... 171
Black Bean Salsa ... 172
Almond and Vegetable Stir Fry ... 173
Caramelized Onions ... 174
Cranberry Barbecued Chicken ... 175
Barbecued Chicken and Avocado Salad ... 177
Chicken Quesadilla ... 178
Macadamia Mahi Mahi ... 179
Baked Salmon ... 181
4-Ingredient Cheese Biscuits ... 183
Cheesy Garlic Bread ... 184
Gourmet Grilled Cheese Sandwich ... 185
Zebra Crème Brûlée ... 186
Hot Fudge Sauce ... 187
Caramel Sauce ... 188
Chocolate Gravy ... 189

Ever Onward and Upward

192 Living My Best Life

194 Adversity Can Be Your Friend

196 Friends, Faith, and Fortitude

199 See You in Heaven

208 Age Gracefully

212 What's Next?

260 About the Author

261 Thank you, Duke Mansion

Friends and Family Favorite Recipes

Elizabeth's Spinach Dip . . . 214
Margaret's Bacon Buttery Bites . . . 215
Sweet and Spicy Roasted Pecans . . . 216
Lemon Nutmeg Scones . . . 217
Linda's Chicken and Vegetable Soup . . . 218
Watermelon Mango Salad . . . 220
Holiday Rosemary Grapefruit . . . 222
Spring Green Salad with Berries and Avocado . . . 223
Michael's Red Chicken . . . 224
Michael's White Chicken . . . 225
Bloomin' Onion Quiche with Goat Cheese and Thyme . . . 226
Crispy Baked Parmesan Chicken . . . 228
Barbecued Meatloaf . . . 229
Elizabeth's Creamy Gruyère Chicken . . . 230
Slow-Cooked Barbecued Pork Tenderloin . . . 233
Make-Ahead Sausage and Egg Casserole . . . 234
Fresh Shrimp Salad . . . 235
Roasted Brussels Sprouts . . . 236
Gingered Asparagus with Cashews . . . 237
Broccoli Salad . . . 238
Tomato Cheese Pie . . . 239
Cheese Grits . . . 240
Elizabeth's Mac and Cheese . . . 241
Almond Joy Cake . . . 242
Chocolate Chess Pie . . . 243
Annette's Brownies . . . 244
DeDe's Messy Pie . . . 246
OREO Cookie Freeze . . . 248
Perfect Pecan Pie . . . 249
Pink Things . . . 250
My Favorite Rum Cake . . . 251
Special Day Dessert . . . 253
Troutman Pound Cake and Teddy Bears . . . 254
Smoothies . . . 257
Ultimate Cheesecake . . . 258
Rita's Baked Apple Pie Shake . . . 259

Foreword

The Spotlight

The subtitle of this book references the spotlight. The spotlight is where the director wants you to focus your eyes and ears. It highlights the performer and creates negative space to ignore. You know someone is special when they're under a spotlight.

When my generation was growing up, our favorite performers were in spotlights. We saw our TV stars, movie stars, and rock stars in their element. We didn't see their full lives, but we invited them to be a part of our lives, almost like they were our friends.

This is especially true of our local stars, the ones we were proud were "ours." The news anchor, the lawyer on the billboards, the talented band that played at all of the parties—these were shared people and experiences among those from a particular time and place. When we meet others from our hometowns, we can immediately connect around these touch points that only we know. There's magic in someone being a star to you but a stranger to others.

My sister and I grew up with a TV mom in the local spotlight. As a kid, going to a Charlotte grocery store with my mom was like going to Liverpool with Paul McCartney. But at the grocery store in another city, she was just a regular shopper. Those trips were much faster. To my sister and me, we just had a regular mom whose job included making a new dish every day. But others saw her in a different way. That was hard to understand as a little kid. But looking back, it's fun knowing that someone in

our family taught a generation how to cook and set an example for how to go for what you want.

Today, there are no more spotlights on prominent people. Instead, there are floodlights. Floodlights show us the grime, the junk, the dust. Floodlights show us everything around a person whether we want to see it or not (and whether they want us to see it or not). Floodlights take away the specialness.

I'm so thankful that my mom's TV career was in the spotlight era. This book is a throwback to that time. It's intended to be comfortable, informative, and for my mom to share some of what she's learned in a life well-lived. And, of course, it's intended to share so many recipes that have helped define her and many of our family's best moments.

Some of you may have never heard of my mom until you saw this book. I hope you'll agree that it casts a spotlight on who I think is a pretty impressive woman.

Michael Stutts

Introduction

Coming Home

I grew up in a tiny Southern town sheltered from any kind of big city activity—spent my days playing alone and entertaining myself with my imagination at my grandparents' farm in the middle of nowhere.

How did I go from there to riding in a helicopter in Hawaii hovering over an active volcano spewing lava ... standing on a glacier in Alaska a little nervous about falling into a giant crevice ... gazing over brilliant fields of tulips as far as the eye could see in Holland ... watching diamonds being cut in Belgium, the diamond capitol ... walking the red carpet at the Grammys in Los Angeles ... riding a professional polo pony in Jamaica ... meeting Michael Jackson face to face, inches apart ... telling Andy Griffith that I grew up in a real Mayberry ... sitting one-on-one with superstar Debbie Reynolds (who will always be Tammy to me) and learning about her struggles and lessons learned ... spending the day with legendary fashion designer Oscar de la Renta ... riding on the back of a motorcycle on a major NASCAR track with a NASCAR star ... attending world premieres and parties for blockbuster movies ... chatting with "James Bond" in London ... interviewing major movie stars, musicians, and newsmakers from around the world ... appearing on two soap operas ... discovering I am related to royalty ... and many more adventures over the decades of being on television? How did I end up reporting on TV? It came about through faith, dreams, my always-believing-in-me mom, and *food.* My love of food took me on an incredible journey.

Fresh from the Field

Just like many of my favorite foods, my journey started in farm country. Growing up in a small community gave me a strong foundation for which I am profoundly grateful.

Reflections

Farm to Fork....................4
Food Means Family 6
An Unexpected Hero 8
The Magic of Show Biz 10
Earning My Wings.......... 14
New England 17
Teaching on Tobacco Road ...19
Headed to Charlotte 24
Big Miracles in
Tiny Packages..............26
Mother Knows Best..........33

Farm to Fork

As a child, all the food I knew was organic, long before organic was cool. Milk, eggs, meat, fresh fruits, and fresh vegetables came from my grandparents' farms in rural Cleveland County, North Carolina, and Cherokee County, South Carolina. When my parents moved "to town" (tiny Shelby, North Carolina), our farm-raised food was supplemented with my father's amazing and much-admired garden treasures. I *still* hear from people who were the beneficiaries of his huge garden and huge heart. We always had an abundant garden and shared with everyone we knew and some we didn't.

Daddy taught me that you don't pick the corn until the water is boiling, and you don't pluck the tomato until the bread is generously slathered with Duke's Mayonnaise to give it "a little twang," as they say. (If you aren't already familiar with Duke's Mayonnaise, do yourself a favor and visit dukesmayo.com.) The time from vine to plate should be as short as possible. When Daddy sent me to the garden, he told

When Daddy sent me to the garden, he told me I could walk there, but as soon as I picked those delicious vegetables and fruits, I was to run back to the kitchen.

I was also blessed to be surrounded by the best cooks to prepare that food. They did not go to fancy cooking schools. They learned from their moms and dads using the best simple ingredients.

me I could walk there, but as soon as I picked those delicious vegetables and fruits, I was to *run* back to the kitchen. And if I fell down, I had to start all over again because that wasted crucial time.

I was also blessed to be surrounded by the best cooks to prepare that food. They did not go to fancy cooking schools. They learned from their moms and dads using the best simple ingredients—all organically grown and prepared with lots of real butter and real cream and with simple herbs and spices.

Those of you who have watched me over the years have heard me talk about my beautiful, fashionable mom who was also amazing in the kitchen. Congressman Jack Hunt, a family friend who served our country as a congressman, called me the day my mama went to heaven. He said that in all his travels eating in fancy restaurants around the world, no one was a better cook than my mama. Jack was ninety-four years old when he told me that.

Even with this food-focused background and love of TV, my journey to multiple entertainment TV shows, travel features, interviews with stars, cooking shows, and five cookbooks was not a straight line. As much as I loved television and food, I had no formal broadcasting or cooking education or experience. I never even imagined getting the chance to do what I have loved now for years. That opportunity came about in the most unlikely, unexpected, unusual ways.

Food Means Family

Food was the focus for every gathering, large or small, for my family and our many friends. Joyful family gatherings took place often, as did casual entertaining of close family friends. Every day, a parade of friends would drop by our house—which was never locked, even on vacation—to enjoy talking, laughing, and especially eating my mom's delicious cooking, or to pick a few vegetables from my father's garden. Not a day went by that we didn't have something yummy to share, especially delicious, decadent desserts.

Coming from a large extended farming family on my mom's side, we had reunions throughout the year along with the many church homecomings and birthday celebrations. My grandmother and her father, my great-grandfather, were born on the same day, so every October we celebrated their birthdays (he lived to be well into his nineties) with her eleven brothers and sisters and their offspring. The fall weather was always crisp and beautiful. Huge tables were filled with the most fantastic food. Even as a small child, I remember how proud I felt that my many relatives seemed to "stalk" the section of the table where my mom unpacked and placed her delicious dishes. Her food was gone in an instant.

My father's side of the family was much smaller, and while we didn't have large gatherings, we had plenty of good food. From the time I was a toddler, I took part in harvesting food. I picked strawberries, blueberries, apples, peaches, watermelons, and cantaloupes. I wasn't very good at picking corn, but I sure did love running through the maze while my grandmother plucked the corn. My favorite farm activity was gathering eggs, like an Easter egg hunt every day. To this day, I am fascinated by hens laying eggs, and I would have a chicken and a rooster right now if I could. And all my favorite foods seem to star *eggs* as the main ingredient—quiche, souffles, eggs benedict, custards, puddings, pies, and cakes.

On the subject of my ancestors, there is a surprising and interesting little twist. Because of my hundreds of cooking segments, a spin-off cooking show, and five cookbooks, I was often introduced at speaking engagements as "Charlotte's Martha Stewart." While I interviewed the real recipe, garden, and craft queen three times, I certainly did not compare myself with her, the homemaking guru of the world.

In 2017, almost forty years since I began my broadcasting career, my son, Michael, gave me Ancestry.com as my Mother's Day gift. While researching my past, I learned that my great-grandmother on my father's side was named Martha Stewart. No relation as far as I know, but it was certainly what I refer to as a "God-wink"—a delightful little encounter or experience that may seem coincidental but is so astonishing that is has to be a sign of divine intervention. There have been so many of those in my life since I have acknowledged them for what they really are.

My favorite farm activity was gathering eggs, like an Easter egg hunt every day. To this day, I am fascinated by hens laying eggs, and I would have a chicken and a rooster right now if I could.

An Unexpected Hero

When I was eleven years old, a tragedy took place that had a profound impact on the rest of my life. As it turns out, one of my heroes is my little brother, David.

While out riding his bicycle on a busy road—there were no bike paths back then—he was struck by a truck and critically injured. My parents were told he would not make it through the night. When he was still with us the following morning, my parents were told that even if he made it through another day, with the severe injury to his brain and his deep coma, he would have permanent brain damage and, as they described it at the time, would be "a vegetable."

It was the last day of school, and the principal called an assembly in the auditorium to warn every child about the dangers of riding bikes. Everything about that somber gathering and the entire summer was traumatizing. My parents spent every day at the hospital. Family friends took me in for two months and provided meals for my parents.

After thirty-eight days, to the shock of every health professional that had been called in from across the state, my brother woke up. The prognosis remained grim. He could not walk or talk and had to learn everything all over again. They were certain he would never be normal. After forty-four days in the hospital, he went home to start life again like an infant even though he was eight years old.

Through much prayer and hard work, he was allowed to start back to school in the fall though his physical challenges were daunting. Children can be very cruel. For the rest of his public-school years, from age eight to eighteen, he was made fun of and teased as he worked to learn everything all over again. Among his challenges was having double vision. Imagine seeing *two* of every word on a page and everything around you. Even so, he was determined to be victorious over his disabilities. And he *was*—in gigantic ways.

Through a renewed faith in God, the many prayers of friends and family, and his raw grit, my brother showed everyone what a miracle looks like. He went on to college, returned to our hometown, became an extraordinarily successful businessman, and turned his "mess into his message." He traveled and spoke out against bullying. When our hometown's major industries went overseas and our main street became rundown, he transformed our town into a shining example of how to survive through hardship. He restored and repurposed the buildings, and brought the town square back to life with shops, museums, concerts, and award-winning restaurants. Along

I gained a faith foundation that has sustained me and kept me strong since that day many decades ago.

with his successful real estate and building business, he was the chairman of a bank and used his financial success generously to make a difference in many lives. He now serves on the City Council and is a major force in making our hometown thrive.

Throughout David's ordeal, I saw miracles take place over and over. I gained a faith foundation that has sustained me and kept me strong since that day many decades ago. I continue to see the miracles happening in his life and mine. Genesis 50:20 tells us that what was meant for evil, God can make good.

The Magic of Show Biz

My love and appreciation for food was matched only by my passion for TV, movies, and music. I spent my childhood days dreaming, imagining, and playing alone. I watched TV for hours every day, went to the movies with my grandmother at least two afternoons a week, and listened to the music my father loved when I wasn't watching TV or going to movies.

While in the Navy, my father was based in New York where he spent a lot of time going to nightclubs and shows, which influenced his love of music. His favorites were the big bands and popular performers of his day, from Frank Sinatra to Elvis. That music was piped throughout our house. His mom played the banjo in a country western band. This all gave me such admiration for performers in every genre.

One of my favorite shows was *The Mickey Mouse Club*. I *really* wanted to be a Mouseketeer, but I didn't get the singing and dancing genes as much as I wished I did. I loved "show business," but living in a small Southern town gave me little hope of ever making it a reality in my life. But without realizing it, those passions and dreams were subtly playing a role in my future. Some of my most memorable dream-come-true moments as an adult were made more meaningful because of those childhood experiences and fantasies.

I never got to be a Mouseketeer, but each year I hosted several episodes of my noontime TV show from the Magic Kingdom at Disney World in Florida.

It was magical. I interviewed Mickey Mouse, Goofy, and Donald Duck. The animator for Bambi and Thumper drew pictures especially for me to take home. I got to meet and interview the current Disney stars. And I got to take my own very young children to this magical place where I was actually *working*.

I also adored the *I Love Lucy* TV show. Lucille Ball made me really want a career in TV, but again, I knew that was so very unlikely. I never got to meet her but was thrilled when I got to interview her daughter, Lucy Arnaz. Lucy Jr. was not interested in talking about her mom as much as I wanted to hear about her mom. So that interview did not go particularly well, but it still has a special place in my heart because

her mom entertained and inspired me for so many years. When I finished the interview, my good friend and director Chuck Maye quietly said through my earpiece, "I *don't* love that Lucy."

Debbie Reynolds was a superstar. I could watch *Singin' in the Rain* every day, but the movie that had the biggest impression on me was *Tammy and the Bachelor*. For whatever reason, I loved that movie and played her "Tammy" 45 vinyl record over and over. Many years later, Debbie Reynolds came to Charlotte, and I was assigned to interview her. I could hardly sleep the night before. I was totally starstruck when she entered the studio. She came early, and we had time to visit. I got to tell her how much I loved her and her work.

After the live interview, I expected my idol to be whisked away in her limousine back to the Land of the Stars. As I was finishing my show with tosses, teases, interviews, and cooking segments, I looked over, and Debbie Reynolds was *still there*, observing from the darkened studio on the other side of the bright TV lights shining in my direction. She stayed. After the show, she asked if we could just talk. She seemed to have honed-in on my needs. Her drivers went to lunch, but she stayed with me for hours, asked about my life, and then shared her stories, struggles, and victories, somehow sensing that I needed to listen and learn from her bad decisions. I loved her even more and felt so blessed that another childhood dream just happened.

Years later, I got to meet Tammy's love, the bachelor in that movie, Leslie Nielson. He was no longer the romantic lead that I had a little crush on because Tammy did. He was the star of *The Naked Gun* and had become a huge comedy star. I met and interviewed him first in Hollywood before the premier for *The Naked Gun*. He was so kind to me. He and the movie producer, David Zucker, came to Charlotte, and we spent more time laughing together. I love people who make me laugh, and he was very good at it. I am giggling as I write this.

Thinking of *The Naked Gun* triggers one of my most special memories. When I was nine years old, my father and I took a road trip to visit relatives in Memphis. As we headed home, we drove by a home with a huge yard, beautiful trees, and a gate with guitars on it. *Hmm, whose house could that be?*

My father, who knew no strangers, decided to stop. We pulled up to the gate, and Elvis's Uncle Vester strolls over. He and my father had a good ol' boy conversation, and the next thing I knew, we were sitting in big chairs under a big tree with a big motorcycle zooming around. The young man on the motorcycle stopped to say a polite hello and then sped away. He would wave again from time to time as he vroomed around his spacious thirteen-acre yard. Yes, at age nine I met Elvis Presley at Graceland.

While in the Navy, my father was based in New York where he spent a lot of time going to nightclubs and shows, which influenced his love of music. His favorites were the big bands and popular performers of his day, from Frank Sinatra to Elvis.

My nine-year-old-self was not like nine-year-olds today who are already gaga over rock stars. I was far more interested in playing with his cute dog and could not help but be curious about why his mother would let him ride his massive motorcycle on the grass.

Fast forward a few decades: I was back visiting Memphis, all grown up and working for a TV station interviewing stars of the movie *Memphis Belle.* I went back to visit Graceland and found the once-secluded, private, Southern residence had become a major tourist attraction with trams and souvenir trinkets. I liked my sweet, Southern childhood memories better, but in the very busy gift shop, I found a cookbook with Elvis's favorite recipes compiled by Uncle Vester, the man who befriended my father and me all those years ago. I came home with a copy. There I found a fantastic pound cake recipe but thought it disrespectful to put this treasured recipe on my TV show without permission. I just kept my memories and the pound cake recipe to myself.

A year later, I was interviewing Priscilla Presley for *The Naked Gun 2 1/2.* Before they turned on the cameras, she and I had a delightful conversation about my childhood visit to Graceland, her newlywed home. We enjoyed sharing memories of a place so special to her. Priscilla is a gracious and lovely woman. While Uncle Vester was the guard at Graceland during my childhood, the changing of the guard put Priscilla in charge, and she kindly gave me permission to share the pound cake recipe. Even though I have prepared dozens of different pound cake recipes on TV, this one is my favorite.

So many other adventures have made this small-town girl so grateful, but I haven't told you yet how I got my dream job even after a disastrous audition.

Earning My Wings

My life moved along in the predictable pattern of Southern girls of my era. I graduated from high school and made my debut in the beautiful white dress I assured my parents could also be my wedding dress. That one-time-worn dress recently went to Goodwill along with the wedding dress I fell in love with from the cover of a magazine.

After graduating from the University of North Carolina at Chapel Hill, I broke ranks and chose to take off down a road less traveled by young women from small Southern towns. I applied for a job as a stewardess, now called a flight attendant. My first job interview that May, just before my college graduation, was with Eastern Airlines. I got the job a week after earning my bachelor's degree in early childhood development, and off I went to Miami, Florida, for training.

What a culture shock. Miami was nothing like Shelby, North Carolina, and for the first time complete strangers surrounded me in a city that felt like another country. Like so many other times in my life, I wondered

What a culture shock. Miami was nothing like Shelby, North Carolina, and for the first time complete strangers surrounded me in a city that felt like another country.

if I'd bitten off a little more than I could chew.

I experienced so many things for the first time during those six weeks of training. Along with learning how to ditch an airplane over the ocean, treat someone with a heart attack, handle unruly passengers, serve drinks during turbulence, and other important skills in the sky, we were taught modeling and beauty regimens by New York modeling agencies. They held us to very high standards and were measured and weighed in each day. Since I was five feet, seven inches tall and weighed 115 pounds, I wasn't worried—but I should have been. The instructors told me that my hips were an inch too large for the rest of me (they still are, by the way), and I had to lose that inch before I could graduate and become a stewardess. They measured me every day, and that inch did not budge, no matter how little I ate or how much I exercised. I felt like a failure.

During one of the daily tape measure tests, a new instructor from *Harper's Bazaar* magazine was evaluating us. I can still see her beautiful face when she turned to the other instructors and said, "This girl can't lose another inch in her hips. She is built like this." I was so relieved and hopeful that

I could still earn my wings with a larger-than-allowed bottom. I got those wings and went to work, but—I kid you not—at least once a week I was weighed and measured at airports around the country to make sure I did not add even a millimeter to that inch. I smile as I remember this, knowing how those oppressive rules and standards have dramatically changed for women. I still cringe a little when I see a tape measure.

Rigid rules, strange hours, airport hotels, and not really enjoying flying all that much made this job a one-year-only adventure.

In August, I married Clyde Stutts II, my boyfriend since childhood, and moved to Newport, Rhode Island, where he was stationed in the United States Navy. Three weeks later, Clyde was deployed for nine months.

As Christmas approached, I could hardly wait to go home and visit my family after being all alone in Newport for five months. On December 23, my flight to Charlotte originated in Boston (the nearest airport to Newport). The biggest snowstorm of my life, even to this day, poured down on Boston, and all flights were canceled. I spent the night on the floor of Boston Logan International Airport holding on to hope that I could get home the next day, Christmas Eve. I was crushed to learn that all flights on December 24 were completely booked. I would not get home in time for Christmas and had no way to get back to Newport.

Out of desperation, I went to the Eastern Airlines Crew Lounge and sobbed out my story. A compassionate airline captain made the kind decision to let me "stow away" on the stewardess jump seat since I was trained and knew what to do. I got home in time for Christmas, and to this day, I am grateful that I earned my wings.

New England

As soon as we moved into a new apartment, Clyde left on the USS *Charles H. Roan* for a tour of the Mediterranean, and I started life as a navy wife and third-grade teacher in Newport. My navy lieutenant husband was deployed for most of the two years I spent in New England. While I promised to kiss the ground if I could just get back to my Southern roots and warm weather, I genuinely loved my time learning the New England culture. Every Sunday I would hike the Cliff Walk by myself and imagine the life of those living in the magnificent mansions along that rocky shore.

Because I was alone again, surrounded by no one I knew, I was forced to find new friends and fit in. While the dazzling mansions along the Cliff Walk were mesmerizing, they did not represent the majority of New Englanders. While cliquish and cautious at first, once you earn their trust, they are genuine friends forever—as proud of their heritage as I am of mine.

I learned that the people of the Old South and New England have many similar traits, including deep accents that required repeating or explaining what we were saying. When I was teaching third grade, I had to have one of my students call out the spelling words. My sweet third graders were phonetically spelling the words when I

While I promised to kiss the ground if I could just get back to my Southern roots and warm weather, I genuinely loved my time learning the New England culture.

---

called them out, so they had extra syllables and letters—*nouw* instead of now, *heulp* instead of help, and *dawg* instead of dog.

Southerners and New Englanders share many strong faith and family values, quaint towns, beautiful nature, and great regional food. I was the appreciative recipient of warm New England hospitality and fabulous food. My Southern food heritage made me a fast learner in preparing their versions of favorite foods. We both like the simple recipes with quality ingredients

and using the foods native to the area. I still enjoy the marvelous traditional recipes I learned from them (the "Lobster Rolls" on page 75 and the "New England Clam Chowder" on page 76) and recall so fondly the people who welcomed me and showed me their history, habits, and way of life.

Southerners and New Englanders share many strong faith and family values, quaint towns, beautiful nature, and great regional food.

Teaching on Tobacco Road

After his military service, Clyde enrolled in graduate school back in Chapel Hill. I would provide for us while he earned his MBA. The only thing I knew how to do and was trained for was teaching school, but with so many other wives working to put their husbands through school, I knew getting a job would not be easy. I was thrilled when I was hired as a sixth-grade teacher at a school in nearby Durham, North Carolina, happy to make the commute.

Though only ten miles apart, Chapel Hill and Durham were very different towns—and still are in many ways. You've probably heard of the famous Tobacco Road basketball rivalry between the UNC Tarheels and Duke Blue Devils. The differences go deeper than that though. Chapel Hill grew around and was sustained by the university. Its population was not very diverse unless you count the age differences between students and professors. Durham grew and then declined with the tobacco and textile industries and then grew again as the city invested in new industries and repurposed the old industrial buildings. Home to the nation's first fully independent Black community, the Hayti district, Durham had a large Black community and ran the gamut of socioeconomic classes.

Driving just ten miles from Chapel Hill to Durham for work was like riding a roller coaster through a cross section of America. I passed millionaires and paupers, stately old mansions and crumbling mill houses, cow pastures

Ultimately, teaching these precious students was rewarding, blessed, and memorable. I learned more about life from them than they did from me.

and industrial smokestacks, mom and pop soda shops, and sprawling shopping centers. This roller-coaster experience was sometimes shocking and heart-wrenching and at other times joyful and funny.

Excited and thankful for this hard-to-come-by job, I cheerfully showed up for my first day of work. I discovered that my school was ancient, run down, and in the middle of a similarly neglected housing project. My classroom was in a small, separate structure away from the main building. The three other sixth-grade teachers and I met to read our roster of students. The other teachers were veterans of this school and began sharing frightful stories of encounters with certain students. With each story, they would name the student and ask, "Who got *him*?" or "Who has *her*?" To my dismay, every single one of those students with discipline problems had been placed in the *new* teacher's classroom—*mine*. I suppose their logic was to put all the troublemakers in one place, so the other three sixth-grade classrooms would have fewer disruptions.

Ultimately, teaching these precious students was rewarding, blessed, and memorable. I learned more about life from them than they did from me. It's been four decades since that job, and I still think about those children with such awe, love, and respect. Their lives were so complicated. Our ages were not that far apart since I was in my early twenties and they were early teens, but they had experienced things that I have never had to endure.

Among the lowlights of that year were three murders involving immediate family members of students in my class. On one occasion, I was called to the office to take a phone call from a student's mother. She was in jail for committing murder the night before and asked that I make sure none of the other students were unkind to her daughter who was in school that day after witnessing the murder at her home the night before. I assured the mom I would protect her child. Her daughter spent much of the day giving details of the murder to everyone in my classroom. I wasn't sure how to handle that. It had not been a part of my UNC Chapel Hill education.

Several of my sixth graders could not read. How they got to sixth grade without that foundational skill is a story for another time. So while I realized early on that while the "three *R*s" (reading, writing, and arithmetic) needed to be covered every day, my unique classroom really needed to learn about love, getting along, and the importance of getting an education. Before we could accomplish any of that, however, we needed to learn some discipline and self-control. We embarked on some positive behavior reinforcement using two things that have always motivated me—food and music. I rewarded positive behavior and tried my best to ignore bad behavior unless someone's life was endangered.

My students and I loved Michael Jackson. (I still do. Getting to meet him in person later seemed like this part of my life coming full circle.) When our classroom had a "good day," I played Michael Jackson music at the end of the day, and the kids would dance, dance, dance, and sing. I loved it as much as they did.

An equally effective strategy was rewarding good behavior with food. I had no idea how powerful delicious food could be. I divided my class into teams. Every day, I kept a score pad. Every kind, thoughtful, good action by a student earned their team a point. Every bad action lost a point. On Friday afternoons, the best team got to have a little party of sorts with homemade treats I brought in.

It always made me a little sad to see the others watch the winning team, but you can bet I made sure the rewards were spread around by moving the "leader." I observed that each team seemed to have one student that kept everybody motivated to "be good." Throughout the entire week, every time there was a notable good deed or a not so good deed, I would pick up the "scorepad," and suddenly you could hear a pin drop as I announced what points were being added or deleted. While modifying their behavior, they also seemed to enjoy the competition. Before long, the whole class was celebrating a tie—a win for all. We ate fun, yummy food and listened to Michael Jackson. And learning was taking place all the while.

I think back so fondly of how truly smart and savvy they all were. I thank God for the patience, love, understanding, and solutions to help them. All these years later, I still giggle at some of the funny, poignant, and joyful things that happened that year. One moment in particular stands out.

We had a lot of visitors to our classroom—education administrators, supervisors, teachers and principals from other schools, and social workers. I candidly explained to my sixth graders the importance that we "perform" well whenever we had visitors. We never knew exactly when guests were coming, but we could hear voices and crunching gravel as the observers made their way to our outbuilding away from the rest of the school. My kids were awesome every time. They knew just what to do.

We always looked like the model classroom, and they really got into it. They would raise their hands—raising hands instead of shouting out was a new skill. They would say things like, "Oh, Mrs. Stutts, I really love this new math you taught me. It helps me every day." It was all I could do to keep from bursting out laughing. We all had twinkles in our eyes and the little smiles of coconspirators. We were *good*. Soon, that good behavior and excitement to learn became automatic.

The biggest breakthrough came when the marvelous Durham County music teacher suggested that we channel their interests and energy into a production. She collaborated with me to produce a musical. We rehearsed every day for months. It was pure joy for all of us. Everyone knew about my "special" classroom, and when we premiered our entertainment

I was awarded Teacher of the Year, which should have gone to my precious students who proved that "troublemaker" label was wrong. They really taught me more than I taught them. They were smart, hard workers and awesome performers who embraced the rewards of effort, hope, optimism, cooperation, encouragement, accomplishment, and other life lessons.

extravaganza showcasing the amazing talent in my classroom, people could hardly believe it. To this day, my eyes fill up with tears of pride and joy seeing what those kids accomplished in one year. It was phenomenal. People came from all over the county to see these transformed students who had developed quite a reputation at such a young age.

I was awarded Teacher of the Year, which should have gone to my precious students who proved that "troublemaker" label was wrong. They really taught me more than I taught them. They were smart, hard workers and awesome performers who embraced the rewards of effort, hope, optimism, cooperation, encouragement, accomplishment, and other life lessons.

Headed to Charlotte

These next few years would determine what was ahead for the remaining decades of my life. Clyde completed graduate school and began the interview process for his first job. With an MBA, it could be anywhere in the world. I did some serious praying for it to be Charlotte, a city close to my Southern roots and the people I had known my whole life. My husband's priority was a good job wherever it happened to be.

I did some serious praying for it to be Charlotte, a city close to my Southern roots and the people I had known my whole life.

My prayers were answered. After many interviews, Hugh McColl (the banking legend) sent a private plane to Chapel Hill to pick up Clyde and fly him to Charlotte for an interview. Recently, someone who worked for Mr. McColl at that time told me that he tossed his car keys to her that fateful day decades ago and said, "Drive Clyde around the best places in Charlotte and make sure he takes this job." He did.

Then I began looking for a teaching job. Again, the McColls played a huge role in our future. They and other important city leaders had recently started a new private school in Charlotte with a strong academic focus. Charlotte Latin School is now one of the best schools in the country. They were looking for a language arts specialist. Just before my second year in the Durham County School system, a position opened for a language arts specialist. The requirements were eight years of teaching experience and a master's degree in education. I had neither of those but got the job anyway. That experience qualified me for the wonderful new job at Charlotte Latin. It felt like God was working in His mysterious ways for me.

I became the language arts specialist for grades one through six for this school of high achievers. It was culture shock coming from Braggtown. Charlotte Latin had no discipline problems. Every child was well behaved, prepared, highly motivated, and learning above their grade level. My challenge at this school was to keep them interested and engaged and to assure their parents—most all with graduate degrees—that I was taking their children to the next level of their education.

Thankfully, my role was not so much the basics but the enrichment. So once again, I got to teach creatively. The children at Charlotte Latin were bright, fun, and eager to please. I loved every minute. It was interesting that, yet again, my classroom was away from the main part of the school. So when my students, ages six years to twelve years, traipsed out to my trailer, I wanted to make it fun and unpredictable. We did lots of creative writing, and again, I loved bringing treats to class.

It felt like God was working in His mysterious ways for me.

I still have the joy of seeing and hearing from many of them. When I run into them in a variety of places—restaurants, church, parties, malls, games—with a smile, I tell them to introduce me to their current family and friends by saying, "We were in elementary school together," omitting the part that I was their teacher. I have remained lifelong friends with many of them and their parents.

My second year at Charlotte Latin was my last year of teaching because another huge prayer was answered.

Big Miracles in Tiny Packages

Like many women, I always dreamed of having children. While I enjoyed teaching other people's children, I desperately wanted my own. I felt it was truly my calling in life to be a mom. I was devastated when it seemed I couldn't conceive. I went to many doctors, went through multiple operations for endometriosis, endured tests and painful procedures, and finally began fertility drugs. My doctors were wonderful but sadly told me it would be a true miracle if I had a child. They said I needed to accept that I probably would not. *I did not accept that.* I just kept praying.

Suddenly, to the genuine shock of my doctors, a pregnancy test turned up positive. They sat me down and said that I must face reality, not to get too excited because they didn't think I could possibly make it through the pregnancy successfully. *I remained excited.*

The academic year at Charlotte Latin wrapped up in early June, and the baby was due in September, actually on Labor Day. My plan was to spend the summer getting everything ready and then become a full-time, stay-at-home mom. I read all the baby books and followed all the instructions enjoying every moment. I didn't know whether I was having a girl or boy, but it didn't matter. We were having a baby.

I was so eager for the big arrival, and apparently so was the baby. A beautiful, healthy baby girl, Elizabeth, arrived three weeks early. I had an unmedicated birth with no complications. I sat in the delivery area of the hospital, within an hour of my baby girl arriving, calling everybody I knew. I not only felt fine, especially with no drugs in my system, but also was filled with energy, excitement, and gratitude. She was so perfect and continues to be to this day.

It was a little strange not going back to school, especially since every fall since first grade I headed to school as a student and then a teacher, but my life was laser focused on my baby girl.

My doctors sat me down for another serious conversation, saying that my underlying fertility issues were still there even though I had a baby. They told me there was really no medical explanation as to why I was able to give birth, and since I had been given such a huge miracle, it would be best if I just focused on being grateful and not trying to have another, meaning no more fertility drugs. At that time, they could have serious side effects later. Not wanting to be greedy with my miracles, I accepted that and went on with life, so thankful to be a mom to my precious little girl. I had started a new career and was busy working and raising my daughter.

Just after Elizabeth turned two, I began to have some worrisome health incidents. I fainted a couple of times and would have waves of nausea. I asked my doctors for a pregnancy test, as unlikely as that was considering my fertility issues. I took the test. They called me from the clinic and said that, as expected, I was not pregnant. But the symptoms continued.

As I prayed about this, I felt peaceful and certain that nothing was wrong

Elizabeth Parker Stutts and Michael Livingston Stutts are the lights and loves of my life.

and that perhaps another miracle had taken place, this time with no medical procedures, surgeries, or drugs. I boldly asked for another pregnancy test and the doctors kindly obliged. This time it was *positive*. Another miracle baby was on the way.

My life at that time was very full and organized, and I wasn't quite sure how I would manage a toddler, an infant, and a full-time job. But I wasn't worried; I was elated. I was about to be the mom of *two* miracle babies. I knew they were so special and would do extraordinary things. I was right. Elizabeth Parker Stutts and Michael Livingston Stutts are the lights and loves of my life.

My smart, mature little girl took charge from day one and did everything like clockwork—checking off every milestone the baby books described earlier than expected. Around eighteen months old, she toddled into my room with a pair of panties and said, "I want to wear big girl pants now." And that was that. We did not have a training stage. She made it easy for me to work and care for her and seemed to know instinctively what she was supposed to do before she was told.

After college she moved to Atlanta and had a huge job with a sports agent in a beautiful corner office of an Atlanta

She is the most organized, productive human I have ever known, and she does it all with such poise, beauty, and grace.

high rise. It was impressive. But then one day out of the blue, she called me and said she was making a big career change. She went from that beautiful office to working in the basement of a church as a youth coordinator. It was so thrilling to watch her make a difference in the lives of those young people. How thankful I am that she not only loved and lived her faith but also led other young people to do the same.

She met her wonderful husband, Brett, and they have been blessed with three incredibly talented, gorgeous children, Reid, Jane, and Brooks. Along with being a mom, she is also an administrator at one of their schools and serves on her church's meal team. She is the most organized, productive human I have ever known, and she does it all with such poise, beauty, and grace. And, yes, she is a fabulous cook. Her fantastic kitchen is a place I love to spend time and enjoy her great food and wonderful company. She counsels me these days.

My life at that time was very full and organized, and I wasn't quite sure how I would manage a toddler, an infant, and a full-time job. But I wasn't worried; I was elated.

Michael, my surprise baby boy, has continued to surprise and delight me every day since he came into the world. He had the most contagious baby laugh that made everyone he met fall in love with him.

When he was barely four, he chose a book from our bookshelf and began to read it out loud. Having taught school, I knew that it was a third-grade reading-level book. I asked Elizabeth if she had been reading it to him—she was seven at the time—thinking that maybe he had memorized it. She said she had never read that book to him. I had, but not enough for him to memorize every word. I chose a new book and handed it to him. He read every word without hesitation. He even read it "in character." Yes, he had taught himself to read by early age four. That was only the beginning. My brilliant little boy, who was as outgoing and funny as he was smart, stunned his teachers and me every day of his life. Elizabeth used to say to me, "Michael is scary smart."

He was also quite an entertainer. He would climb on top of a table, as if mounting a stage with a microphone in hand, and loudly announce, "PRESENTING, MR. MICHAEL." Then he would fling himself to the hardwood floor and onto his knees, right fist high

My brilliant little boy, who was as outgoing and funny as he was smart, stunned his teachers and me every day of his life.

in the air like a rock star. That went on for years.

While he chose not to go into show business, he has attended hundreds of concerts all over the world for those who did. He was the commencement speaker at his high school graduation, and I am still told by people that it was the most entertaining graduation speech ever. After college and graduate school and before going to work in the real world of business, he took a trip around the world seeing and doing things I still have not. While I still think he could be on TV, he performs instead with PowerPoint in client meetings as a management consultant and now works for a big restaurant company in Tampa. It seems fitting that his career is related to food. The apple doesn't fall far from the tree.

Mother Knows Best

One day when Elizabeth was seven months old, my mom came to my home for her weekly visit. I was rocking Elizabeth and watching TV when Mom delivered a straightforward message, said with firm kindness: "I'm worried about you. You have gained weight, you don't wear make-up, and you are letting yourself go. You look terrible, and you need to get out and do something with yourself." She pointed to the TV and said, "That's what you can do." She then picked up the phone book, looked up the number for WBTV, handed me the phone, and said, "Call for an interview."

The strangest part of that whole episode is that I did not resist. My mother gave me a command, and I obeyed. I wanted to honor her wish and truthfully felt certain that would be the end of it—one of the most successful TV stations in the world would certainly not make an appointment with a stranger over the phone.

My mother's reasoning was that since the most beloved woman in television at that time, Betty Feezor, had passed away, there seemed to be a need for someone to share recipes, crafts, and lifestyle information. My mother had no concerns about the fact that I had absolutely no television experience other than tap dancing on TV when I was four years old.

Her confidence in me was based on my love of food. Throughout my Newport and Chapel Hill days, I had further developed my cooking skills. I shared recipes in a newsletter I created for my teacher colleagues,

The Stutts family at the dinner table: Clyde, Barbara and daughter Elizabeth. (Elmer Horton Photo)

Barbara Stutts says her mom got her off to the right start

served on food committees for several philanthropic organizations, and belonged to dinner clubs that involved creating and experiencing new cuisines. And I had a rather unusual craft background.

As the breadwinner in Chapel Hill, I earned extra money creating and selling crafts. My "breakthrough earnings," as they say in the financial world, happened when my mother-in-law carried a handbag I had painted for her as a gift. She attended many meetings and conventions nationally and internationally as the wife of the American Bankers Association's treasurer. She was always asked about her bag. Long story short, at night after teaching all day, I sat at our dining room table, which I had also hand painted, and created handbags for women all over the country. My mother decided that qualified me for doing crafts on TV. But creating recipes and crafts in my kitchen by myself was very different from broadcasting them. But my mom believed in me and knew that with God, all things are possible.

Southern Classics

These recipes from my early life sparked my love for good food and fresh ingredients. They're simple to make and easy to master.

Hot Artichoke Dip 36
Mom's Famous Standing Rib Roast 37
Twice-Baked Potatoes 38
Garden Salad and Red Wine Vinaigrette 39
1-2-3-4 Cake 40
Chocolate Frosting for 1-2-3-4 Cake 41
Classic Caramel Frosting for 1-2-3-4 Cake 42
Pineapple Filling and Frosting for 1-2-3-4 Cake 43
Hot Chicken Salad 44
Cranberry Salad 45
Roasted Fresh Asparagus 46
Lemon Chess Pie 47
Sweet Potato Pie 49
Pumpkin Praline Pie 50
Tasty, Tangy Herbed Tomatoes 51
Asparagus New Potato Salad 52
Horseradish Carrots 53
Creamed Fresh Corn 54
Seasoned Corn on the Cob 55
Pasta Primavera 57
Refrigerator Vegetable Slaw 58
Daddy's Boiled Shrimp and Cocktail Sauce 59
Shrimp Creole 61
Baked Alaskan Halibut 62
Homemade Pimento Cheese 63
Vegetable Garden Salad 64
Fresh Apple Cake 65
Cousin's Chocolate Cake 66
Surprise Ham and Cheese Rolls 67
Homemade Chicken Noodle Soup 68
Chicken, Sausage, and Wild Rice Casserole 69
White Bean and Spinach Soup 71
Macaroni Beef Supper 72
Mississippi Corn Bread 73
Easy Lemonade Cake 74
Lobster Rolls 75
New England Clam Chowder 76
Cranberry Pecan Cornbread 77
The Best Brownies EVER 79
Goody Bars 80
Favorite Frosted Sugar Cookies 81

Hot Artichoke Dip

SERVES 8 | PREP 10 minutes | COOK 25 minutes

Ingredients

1 small (8.5-ounce) can artichoke hearts

1 cup mayonnaise

1 cup Parmesan cheese

Dash garlic salt

Paprika for garnish

Slivered almonds for garnish

Crackers or chips

Directions

Mash artichoke hearts with a fork.

Combine them with mayonnaise, Parmesan cheese, and garlic salt. Mix well and spread into a 1½-quart baking dish.

Sprinkle with paprika and slivered almonds.

Bake at 350 degrees for 20 to 25 minutes.

Serve with crackers or chips.

Notes

Keep these handy ingredients on your pantry shelf and easily impress unexpected guests.

Mom's Famous Standing Rib Roast

SERVES 8 | PREP 10 minutes | COOK 2 to 3 hours

Ingredients

1 (6-pound) standing rib roast

Salt and pepper, to taste

1 cup heavy cream

3 to 4 tablespoons prepared horseradish

Directions

Place the roast fat-side up in a shallow roasting pan. Season generously with salt and pepper. Do not add water. Do not cover. Bake at 325 degrees to desired degree of doneness.

Rare: 2¼ hours
Medium: 2½ hours
Well Done: 3¼ hours

If your roast is larger, lengthen the cooking time. When the roast is done, remove from the pan and allow it to rest about 15 to 20 minutes. This makes the roast juicier and easier to cut.

Serve with horseradish cream sauce by whipping one cup of heavy cream and stirring in 3 to 4 tablespoons of prepared horseradish.

Notes

This recipe was my mom's dinner-party favorite. When she passed away, I received a phone call from a family friend who was a congressman and world traveler. We reminisced about my youth, and then he said something I will always remember: "I have been blessed to eat at some fine restaurants and extravagant events, but no one cooked a rib roast like your mom."

Twice-Baked Potatoes

SERVES 8 | PREP 30 minutes | COOK 1 hour

Ingredients

4 baking potatoes

4 tablespoons butter

1 cup sour cream

½ cup whole milk

¾ teaspoon salt

½ teaspoon pepper

1 cup Cheddar cheese, shredded and divided

½ cup chives, divided

½ cup bacon, crisply cooked and chopped (optional)

Directions

Pierce each potato with a fork or knife. Bake at 400 degrees for 45 minutes or until tender. Let cool until easily handled.

Cut warm potatoes in halves lengthwise. Scoop out potatoes, leaving skins intact.

Mix potatoes with butter, sour cream, milk, salt, pepper, half the cheese, and half the chives. Pile the mixture back into the potato skins. Refrigerate.

Before serving, reheat the potatoes at 400 degrees until hot (10 to 20 minutes depending on if they are cold or not). Top with remaining cheese, chives, and (optional) chopped bacon. Heat an additional 5 minutes.

Notes

These can be made ahead of time and kept refrigerated. If refrigerated, increase the reheating time before serving.

Garden Salad and Red Wine Vinaigrette

MAKES ¾ cup | PREP 15 minutes

Ingredients

3 tablespoons red wine vinegar or balsamic vinegar

½ cup extra virgin olive oil

1 teaspoon Dijon-style mustard

1 tablespoon fresh parsley, minced

½ teaspoon salt

½ teaspoon black pepper

2 tablespoons sugar

Salad greens and vegetables (your preferences)

Directions

Combine vinegar, oil, mustard, parsley, salt, pepper, and sugar and mix well. Refrigerate and serve mixed with your favorite salad greens and vegetables.

Notes

1-2-3-4 Cake

SERVES 12 to 16 | PREP 30 minutes | COOK 25 minutes

Ingredients

4 large eggs, separate yolks from whites

1 cup (2 sticks) butter, softened

2 cups sugar

3 cups cake flour

1 tablespoon baking powder

¼ teaspoon salt

1 cup whole milk

1 teaspoon pure vanilla extract

Directions

Beat the egg whites until peaks form and set aside.

Beat the butter and sugar until light and fluffy. Add the egg yolks one at a time, beating well after each until smooth and creamy.

In a separate bowl, combine the flour, baking powder, and salt.

Alternate adding small portions of the flour mixture and the milk to the creamy mixture with the mixer on low speed to combine gently. Add the vanilla extract. Then gently fold the beaten egg whites into the mixture.

Grease and flour 3 (9-inch) cake pans. Divide and spread the batter evenly into the prepared pans.

Bake for about 25 minutes at 350 degrees or until top springs back when touched.

Cool in the pan for 10 minutes. Then turn out onto cake racks to cool completely before frosting.

Notes

Mom's fluffy yellow cake and frostings were her most requested desserts. Besides her special touch, the light texture was because she always used cake flour, never all-purpose. Cake flour is made from soft winter wheat, giving cakes a delicate texture.

Chocolate Frosting for 1-2-3-4 Cake

FROSTS 3 (9-inch) cake layers | PREP 1 hour | COOK 40 minutes

Ingredients

1 cup whole milk

1 cup (2 sticks) butter

3 tablespoons unsweetened cocoa powder

2 cups light brown sugar

1 teaspoon vanilla extract

5 cups (approximately) confectioners' sugar

Directions

In a large heavy saucepan, combine the milk, butter, cocoa, and brown sugar. On low heat, stir frequently until the butter and sugar are melted and all are blended well. Bring to a boil and let bubble for about 1 minute without stirring. Lower heat and simmer until thickened, about 15 minutes, without stirring Remove from heat and cool to lukewarm, about 20 minutes.

Stir in vanilla. Gradually beat in confectioners' sugar until consistency is right for spreading.

Notes

This chocolate frosting may take a little practice because the time and temperatures are not exact every time because of variables ranging from weather to stove calibration, but once perfected, it is worth it.

Classic Caramel Frosting for 1-2-3-4 Cake

FROSTS 3 (9-inch) cake layers | PREP 1 hour | COOK 40 minutes

Ingredients

1 cup (2 sticks) butter

1 cup light brown sugar

1 cup dark brown sugar

½ cup heavy cream

2 teaspoons vanilla extract

4 cups confectioners' sugar

Directions

In a large heavy saucepan, combine the butter, both brown sugars, and heavy cream. On low heat, stir frequently until the butter and sugar are melted and all are blended well. Bring to a boil and let bubble for about 1 minute without stirring. Lower heat and simmer until thickened, about 15 minutes, without stirring. Remove from heat and cool to lukewarm, about 20 minutes.

Stir in vanilla. Gradually beat in confectioners' sugar until consistency is right for spreading.

Notes

Like the chocolate frosting, this caramel frosting may take a little practice because the time and temperatures are not exact every time because of variables ranging from weather to stove calibration, but once perfected, it is worth it.

Pineapple Filling and Frosting for 1-2-3-4 Cake

FROSTS AND FILLS 3 (9-inch) cake layers
PREP 40 minutes | COOK 10 minutes

Ingredients

Filling:

2 tablespoons cornstarch

¼ cup sugar

1 (20-ounce) can crushed pineapple, undrained (about 2½ cups)

4 tablespoons orange juice

Frosting:

½ cup (1 stick) butter, softened

2 cups confectioners' sugar

Zest from 2 fresh oranges

Orange juice, enough to make a spreadable frosting

Directions

For the filling, combine the cornstarch and sugar in a medium saucepan. Mix in the crushed pineapple and orange juice. Cook over medium heat until thickened. Cool to lukewarm. Spread over the top of each layer.

For the frosting, beat the butter and sugar with an electric mixer until smooth and creamy. Stir in the orange peel. Stir in the orange juice a tablespoon at a time until the consistency is right for spreading. Frost the sides of the cake.

Notes

Hot Chicken Salad

SERVES 6 | PREP 20 minutes | COOK 15 minutes

Ingredients

3½ pounds chicken, cooked and chopped (about 3 cups)

3 cups celery, sliced

3 tablespoons lemon juice

3 tablespoons white or yellow onion, finely chopped

1 cup slivered almonds

1 (4-ounce) jar diced pimiento

1½ cups mayonnaise

2 cups dried seasoned bread crumbs

Directions

In a large mixing bowl combine chicken, celery, lemon juice, onion, almonds, and pimiento. Toss well to combine. Mix in the mayonnaise well. Spread into a casserole dish. Top with the bread crumbs.

Bake at 400 degrees until hot, about 15 minutes. If the chicken salad has been made ahead and refrigerated, it will take longer to heat.

Notes

Cranberry Salad

SERVES 12 | PREP 20 minutes

Ingredients

2 envelopes plain gelatin (soften in 2 tablespoons water)

6 ounces cherry-flavored gelatin

2 cups very hot water

2 cups sugar

3 small, whole oranges

2 (14-ounce) cans whole berry cranberry sauce

2 cups pecans, chopped

2 (8-ounce) cans crushed pineapple, drained

Directions

In a large mixing bowl, stir softened gelatin and cherry gelatin into the very hot, almost boiling, water. Stir until completely dissolved. Stir in sugar until dissolved.

Cut oranges into wedges and remove seeds. Chop in a food processor and add to gelatin mixture.

Stir in cranberry sauce, pecans, and drained pineapple. Mix well.

Pour into a 9 x 13-inch dish (or gelatin mold) and chill until serving.

Notes

Don't be put off by the fact that this is made with gelatin. It's there to hold together the abundant cranberries, oranges, and pecans—all healthy and delicious. It can be made days ahead, keeps well in the refrigerator, and goes with poultry, pork, and even grilled cheese sandwiches for lunch.

Roasted Fresh Asparagus

SERVES 12 | PREP 15 minutes | COOK 10 to 15 minutes

Ingredients

3 pounds fresh asparagus

6 tablespoons extra virgin olive oil

½ teaspoon sea salt

½ teaspoon garlic salt

½ teaspoon black pepper

Directions

Remove woody ends of the asparagus. Line a 15 x 10 x 1-inch baking pan with foil. Place asparagus in a single layer on the foil-lined pan. Drizzle with oil. Sprinkle with salt, garlic salt, and pepper.

Bake at 450 degrees for 10 to 15 minutes and serve immediately.

Notes

Lemon Chess Pie

SERVES 6 | PREP 25 minutes | COOK 25 minutes

Ingredients

1 unbaked 9-inch deep-dish pie crust

2 cups sugar

1 tablespoon all-purpose flour

1 tablespoon cornmeal

6 eggs, well beaten

Juice of 3 lemons (about 9 tablespoons)

3 teaspoons freshly grated lemon peel

½ cup (1 stick) butter, melted

Directions

Thaw or unroll the pie crust into a 9-inch deep-dish pie plate.

Combine the sugar, flour, and cornmeal in the large bowl of electric mixer. Beat in the eggs, lemon juice, lemon peel, and melted butter. Pour into the unbaked pie crust.

Bake at 400 degrees for 25 minutes or until filling seems firm.

Notes

Sweet Potato Pie

SERVES 6 | PREP 30 minutes | COOK 45 minutes

Ingredients

3 medium sweet potatoes (about 1 pound)

1 unbaked 9-inch deep-dish pie crust

1½ cups sugar

3 large eggs, beaten

½ cup (1 stick) butter , melted

1 cup whole milk

1 teaspoon vanilla extract

Directions

Bake the sweet potatoes at 350 degrees until tender, about 45 to 60 minutes. Cool and then peel and mash them. Set aside.

Thaw or unroll the pie crust into a 9-inch deep-dish pie plate.

Using an electric mixer, beat the sweet potatoes, sugar, eggs, butter, milk, and vanilla extract until smooth and creamy. Pour the mixture into the unbaked pie crust.

Bake at 375 degrees for 45 minutes.

Notes

Pumpkin Praline Pie

SERVES 6 | PREP 30 minutes | COOK 50 minutes

Ingredients

Filling:

1 unbaked 9-inch deep-dish pie crust

1 (15-ounce can) cooked pumpkin

¾ cup sugar

⅛ teaspoon cinnamon

⅛ teaspoon nutmeg

⅛ teaspoon allspice

1 teaspoon all-purpose flour

2 eggs, beaten

¼ cup whole milk

Pinch salt

Topping:

2 tablespoons butter, melted

½ cup brown sugar

½ cup pecans, chopped

Directions

Thaw or unroll the pie crust into a 9-inch deep-dish pie plate.

Combine the pumpkin, sugar, cinnamon, nutmeg, allspice, flour, eggs, milk, and salt and mix well. Pour mixture into the unbaked pie crust. Bake at 350 degrees for 40 minutes. While baking, combine the butter, brown sugar, and pecans for the topping.

Remove the pie from the oven. Crumble the topping over the pie and bake an additional 5 to 10 minutes.

Notes

My family loves holiday traditions, so of course, we had to have pumpkin pie at Thanksgiving, even though it was far from being a favorite dessert until my mom made it like this. This version is enjoyed by all, especially served with freshly whipped cream or ice cream.

Tasty, Tangy Herbed Tomatoes

SERVES 4 to 8 | PREP 30 minutes | COOK 5 minutes

Ingredients

4 to 8 small to medium tomatoes (depending on the number of people to serve)

Marinade:

⅔ cup vegetable oil

¼ cup balsamic pomegranate vinegar

¼ cup fresh parsley, minced

1 tablespoon thyme, minced

¼ cup Vidalia onion, chopped

1 clove garlic, minced

1 teaspoon salt

¼ teaspoon black pepper

Garnish:

Fresh mozzarella cheese, sliced

Fresh basil leaves

Directions

Scald the tomatoes for one minute in hot boiling water so that the skins will slip off easily. Remove the skins and core of each tomato. Place the tomatoes in a shallow glass dish.

Combine the oil, vinegar, parsley, thyme, onion, garlic, salt, and pepper and mix well. Pour over the tomatoes and chill overnight. Serve whole or sliced with fresh mozzarella cheese garnished with fresh basil leaves.

Notes

This updated recipe comes from my cookbook *Celebrate the Seasons.* My mom and I both served these often, and we were asked for the recipe every time. I updated the recipe by using balsamic pomegranate vinegar and sweet Vidalia onions this time. In this new version, I recommend serving the tomatoes with fresh mozzarella cheese drizzled with the marinade and garnished with fresh basil leaves.

Asparagus New Potato Salad

SERVES 8 | PREP 30 minutes | MARINATE 3 hours

Ingredients

1½ pounds fresh asparagus

1 pound small new potatoes

½ cup water

¼ cup white wine vinegar

¼ cup red onion, chopped

1 ½ teaspoons Dijon-style mustard

1 teaspoon fresh dill weed, chopped

⅛ teaspoon black pepper

Lettuce leaves to line a serving platter

1 hard-cooked egg, chopped

Directions

Remove woody ends of the asparagus. Cook in a small amount of boiling water until tender-crisp, about 6 minutes. Cool and cut into 2-inch pieces. Set aside.

Wash new potatoes and cook in boiling water 15 to 20 minutes or until tender. Drain. Cool and slice.

Combine asparagus and potatoes in a mixing bowl.

In another small bowl, combine the water, vinegar, onion, mustard, dill, and pepper. Whisk together and pour over the vegetables. Marinate in the refrigerator for 3 hours.

Line a serving platter with lettuce. Place the asparagus and potato salad on the lined plate. Top with the chopped egg.

Notes

"Tender-crisp" means you can pierce it with a fork, but it still has some crunch.

Horseradish Carrots

SERVES 6 | PREP 20 minutes | COOK 20 minutes

Ingredients

8 large carrots, sliced and cooked tender-crisp (about 6 cups)

¼ cup water

2 tablespoons white or yellow onion, finely chopped (optional)

2 tablespoons prepared horseradish

½ cup mayonnaise

½ teaspoon salt

¼ teaspoon pepper

Bread crumbs or crushed crackers

2 tablespoons butter, cut into small pieces

Directions

Place carrots into an 8-inch square casserole dish. Combine the water, onions (optional), horseradish, mayonnaise, salt, and pepper. Pour over carrots. Top with bread crumbs or crushed crackers. Dot with butter.

Bake at 350 degrees for 20 minutes.

Notes

Surprisingly, this was my favorite way to eat carrots when I was growing up. Because Daddy grew horseradish in his garden, we had many experimental horseradish dishes.

Creamed Fresh Corn

SERVES 4 | PREP 30 minutes | COOK 15 minutes

Ingredients

4 ears fresh sweet corn, shucked

1 teaspoon sugar

4 tablespoons butter

½ teaspoon black pepper

½ cup heavy cream

½ teaspoon salt

Directions

Cut corn from the cob, scraping the cob to remove the pulp. Combine the corn and sugar and chill for one hour.

Melt the butter in a saucepan over medium heat. Add corn and cook for one minute. Stir in pepper. Gradually stir in the heavy cream. Cook for 10 minutes, stirring frequently. Stir in salt.

Notes

Daddy was well known for growing Silver Queen corn in our huge garden. I still miss picking it, running back home to cook it quickly before it lost any flavor, and especially eating this delicious fresh sweet corn.

Seasoned Corn on the Cob

SERVES 6 | PREP 30 minutes | COOK 20 minutes

Ingredients

6 ears fresh sweet corn, shucked

4 tablespoons butter, melted

2 tablespoons fresh parsley, chopped

1 teaspoon oregano

½ teaspoon garlic powder

Salt and pepper

3 tablespoons Parmesan cheese, grated

Directions

In a large pot, cover the corn with water and heat to boiling. Boil until tender, about 15 minutes. Remove the corn from the water and place in a baking dish. Drizzle butter evenly over each ear of corn. Sprinkle with parsley, oregano, garlic powder, salt and pepper to taste, and cheese. Cover with foil and keep in a warm oven until serving time.

Notes

Pasta Primavera

SERVES 6 | PREP 40 minutes | COOK 10 minutes

Ingredients

4 tablespoons butter

1 small white or yellow onion, chopped

1 garlic clove, minced

½ pound asparagus, trimmed and cut into 1-inch pieces

¼ pound mushrooms, sliced

1 small cauliflower, broken into florets

1 medium zucchini, sliced into rounds

1 carrot, sliced into rounds

1 cup heavy cream

½ cup chicken stock

2 teaspoons fresh basil, chopped

¾ cup frozen peas

½ cup ham, chopped

3 green onions, sliced

Salt and pepper

12 ounces fettuccine, cooked and drained

1 cup Parmesan cheese, grated

Directions

In a large skillet over medium-high heat, melt butter. Sauté onion and garlic for 1 minute. Add asparagus, mushrooms, cauliflower, zucchini, and carrot. Stir-fry for 2 minutes. Add cream, stock, and basil. Bring to a boil and then lower heat and simmer for about 3 minutes. Stir in peas, ham, and green onions. Cook 1 minute more. Season with salt and pepper to taste. Toss with the fettuccine and sprinkle with cheese. Serve immediately.

Notes

You can experiment with different vegetables or meats to accommodate your favorites. Once you get the vegetables chopped and sliced, it goes together very quickly.

Refrigerator Vegetable Slaw

MAKES 1 quart | PREP 25 minutes

Ingredients

½ large green cabbage, chopped

1 cup white or yellow onion, diced

1 large green pepper, chopped

1 large carrot, shredded

1 cup mayonnaise

½ cup sugar

½ cup white wine vinegar

1 teaspoon salt

Directions

Combine the cabbage, onion, pepper, and carrot in a large bowl.

Whisk together the mayonnaise, sugar, vinegar, and salt. Pour over the vegetables and toss to mix. Refrigerate. It's best to prepare the day before serving.

Notes

Daddy's Boiled Shrimp and Cocktail Sauce

SERVES 6 | PREP 30 minutes | COOK 2 minutes

Ingredients

2 pounds shrimp, peeled and deveined

Cold water

1 tablespoon Old Bay Seasoning

1 lemon, quartered

1 teaspoon salt

1 teaspoon whole peppercorns

Sauce:

1 cup ketchup

3 tablespoons prepared horseradish

2 teaspoons Worcestershire sauce

½ teaspoon sugar

1 teaspoon lemon juice

Hot pepper sauce, to taste

Directions

Peel and devein the shrimp. Bring a large pot of cold water to boil. Add the Old Bay Seasoning, lemon quarters, salt, and peppercorns. Add the shrimp and return to a boil. The moment the shrimp begin turning pink (about 1 to 2 minutes), pour into a colander and rinse with cold water. Chill and serve with cocktail sauce.

For the sauce, mix the ketchup, horseradish, Worcestershire sauce, sugar, lemon juice, and hot pepper sauce. Refrigerate. Adjust seasonings to your own taste.

Notes

Shrimp Creole

SERVES 4 | PREP 30 minutes | COOK 15 minutes

Ingredients

- 2 tablespoons butter
- 2 tablespoons bacon drippings
- ½ cup white or yellow onion, chopped
- ½ cup green pepper, chopped
- ½ cup celery, sliced
- 3½ tablespoons all-purpose flour
- ⅓ cup water
- 2 teaspoons sugar
- Salt, to taste
- Hot pepper sauce, to taste
- Garlic powder, to taste
- Chili powder, to taste
- 1 (1-pound) can diced tomatoes
- 2 tablespoons tomato paste
- 2 bay leaves
- 2 tablespoons parsley, chopped
- 1 pound shrimp, peeled, deveined, and freshly cooked
- 4 cups rice, polenta, or grits, cooked

Directions

Melt the butter with bacon drippings in a large Dutch oven or saucepan. Add the onion, green pepper, and celery and sauté for 2 minutes.

Whisk together the flour, water, sugar, salt, hot pepper sauce, garlic powder, and chili powder in a small bowl and set aside.

Add the tomatoes, tomato paste, bay leaves, and parsley to the sautéed mixture and stir well.

Add the whisked mixture to the creole blend in the Dutch oven and stir well. Lower heat and simmer until thickened, approximately 10 minutes.

Stir in freshly cooked shrimp. Adjust seasonings to taste, adding more hot pepper sauce for those who like it hot.

Serve over fluffy rice, creamy polenta, or grits.

Notes

For the best results, *do not* use frozen packaged shrimp.

Baked Alaskan Halibut

SERVES 6 | PREP 20 minutes | COOK 20 minutes

Ingredients

6 halibut fish fillets

1 cup white wine

1 cup sour cream

1 cup mayonnaise

¼ cup white or yellow onion chopped

1 cup sourdough bread crumbs

¾ cup Cheddar cheese, shredded

Directions

Place the fish fillets in a 10-inch baking dish. Pour the white wine over the fish and marinate while you prepare the other ingredients.

Mix the sour cream, mayonnaise, and onion.

Drain away most of the wine, leaving a little in the baking dish with the fish. Spread the creamy mixture over each fish fillet. Sprinkle with bread crumbs. Bake at 400 degrees until fish is cooked throughout, about 20 minutes.

Top with Cheddar during last 2 minutes of baking.

Notes

My daddy collapsed on a fishing boat catching halibut in Alaska. He passed away a short time later. I find comfort in knowing he was doing what he loved near the end of his life. Because that was his favorite pastime, our freezer was always full of mild, tasty Alaskan halibut fillets. I still miss his seafood the way I miss those fresh garden vegetables.

Homemade Pimento Cheese

MAKES 3 cups | PREP 20 minutes | COOK

Ingredients

2 cups Cheddar cheese, shredded and warmed to room temperature

4 ounces cream cheese, cut into pieces and warmed to room temperature

½ cup mayonnaise

¼ teaspoon cayenne pepper

¼ teaspoon onion powder

1 (4-ounce) jar of pimentos, chopped

Salt and pepper, to taste

Directions

Place the Cheddar cheese, cream cheese, mayonnaise, cayenne pepper, and onion powder into a food processor and process just until blended. Scrape into a bowl and stir in the pimentos.

Spread on choice of bread or serve with crackers.

Add salt and pepper to taste.

Notes

Vegetable Garden Salad

SERVES 6 | PREP 25 minutes

Ingredients

1 cup ricotta cheese

¾ cup mayonnaise

2 tablespoons half-and-half

6 cups spinach leaves, torn

4 ounces bleu cheese, crumbled

1 cup carrots, sliced

1 cup fresh mushrooms, sliced

½ cup red onion, chopped

1½ cups greens peas, cooked

2 hard-cooked eggs, sliced

5 slices of bacon, cooked crisply and crumbled

Directions

In a small bowl, combine ricotta, mayonnaise, and half-and-half and mix well.

In a 2½-quart bowl, layer spinach and half of the ricotta mixture, half of the bleu cheese, carrots, mushrooms, onion, peas, and egg slices. Top with the remaining ricotta mixture and bleu cheese. Top with bacon. Refrigerate several hours to blend flavors.

Notes

Fresh Apple Cake

SERVES 12 to 16 | PREP 40 minutes | COOK 1 hour, 20 minutes

Ingredients

3 large eggs

2 cups sugar

1½ cups vegetable oil or melted coconut oil

3 cups all-purpose flour

1 teaspoon baking soda

1 teaspoon cinnamon

1 (8-ounce) package dates, chopped

1 (7-ounce) can flaked coconut

1½ cups pecans, chopped

1 cup maraschino cherries, chopped

2 teaspoons vanilla extract

3 cups fresh Granny Smith or Braeburn apples, chopped

Cream Cheese Frosting (optional):

½ cup (1 stick) butter, softened

1 (8-ounce) package cream cheese, softened

1 teaspoon vanilla extract

1½ cups confectioners' sugar

Directions

Beat the eggs until thickened. Gradually beat in the sugar and oil.

In a separate bowl, combine the flour, baking soda, and cinnamon. Mix a little of this flour mixture with the dates to keep them from sticking. Add the remaining flour mixture and the dates to the egg mixture.

Grease and flour a tube pan. Pour the batter into the prepared pan. Bake at 300 degrees for 1 hour and 20 minutes or until it springs to the touch.

Stir in the coconut, pecans, cherries, vanilla extract and apples.

For the frosting, beat together the butter and cream cheese. Stir in the vanilla extract and blend well. Add confectioners' sugar until spreadable consistency.

Notes

This cake is delicious without a frosting, but the cream cheese frosting makes it decadent.

Cousin's Chocolate Cake

SERVES 12 to 20 | PREP 30 minutes | COOK 30-40 minutes

Ingredients

Batter:

1 box devil's food cake mix

3 large eggs

⅓ cup vegetable oil

1 cup whole milk

Filling:

1 (8-ounce) package cream cheese, softened

2 tablespoons butter, softened

¼ cup sugar

1 tablespoon cornstarch

1 large egg

2 tablespoons whole milk

½ teaspoon vanilla extract

Frosting:

8 tablespoons (1 stick) butter

4 tablespoons unsweetened cocoa powder

6 tablespoons whole milk

1 teaspoon vanilla extract

1 (16-ounce) box or bag of confectioners' sugar

Directions

Prepare the cake batter by combining the devil's food cake mix, 3 eggs, oil, and milk in a mixing bowl. Set aside.

Prepare the filling by beating the cream cheese, butter, sugar, cornstarch, 1 egg, milk, and ½ teaspoon of vanilla extract until smooth and creamy.

Grease and flour 9 x 13-inch cake pan. Pour half of the cake batter into the prepared pan. Pour the filling over the cake batter. Spread the remaining batter over the filling. Bake for 30 to 40 minutes at 325 degrees (until it springs to the touch).

While the cake is baking, prepare the frosting. Bring the butter, cocoa, and milk to a boil. Cool slightly and add the vanilla extract. Gradually stir in the confectioners' sugar. Spread over warm cake.

Notes

My mom had a cousin who was a worthy competitor as "Best Cook" at the family reunions. I loved this cousin's chocolate cake.

Surprise Ham and Cheese Rolls

SERVES 30 | PREP 30 minutes | COOK 10

Ingredients

3 packages of prepared party rolls

2 sticks butter, softened

3 tablespoons prepared mustard

1 teaspoon Worcestershire Sauce

1 medium white or yellow onion, chopped

1 tablespoon poppy seeds

1 pound deli ham, thinly sliced

¾ pound Swiss cheese, thinly sliced

Directions

Party rolls are smaller and not as thick as dinner rolls. Slice rolls through the middle while still connected.

Beat the butter, mustard, and Worcestershire until smooth and creamy. Fold the onion and poppy seeds into the mixture. Spread the tops and bottoms of the rolls with the butter mixture. Add the ham and cheese slices evenly over the rolls. Place the tops over the bottoms. Wrap in foil. Bake at 400 degrees for 10 minutes. If prepared earlier and refrigerated, you will need to bake a little longer.

To serve, cut into individual rolls.

Notes

I call them "surprise" because they are so much better than they sound and not a typical ham and cheese sandwich. This recipe is a perfect example of synergy happening, meaning I am not crazy about the individual ingredients but love what happens when they come together.

Homemade Chicken Noodle Soup

SERVES 6 | PREP 30 minutes | COOK 2 hours

Ingredients

2½ pounds split chicken breasts (with skin and bones)

Water to cover chicken

¼ large white or yellow onion, peeled (about ⅓ cup)

3 celery ribs with leaves

2 carrots, cut into chunks

Salt, to taste

Pepper, to taste

6 ounces uncooked bow tie pasta (half of a 12-ounce box)

⅔ cup celery, sliced

⅔ cup carrots, sliced

1 cup heavy cream

1 tablespoon butter

Directions

Place the chicken breasts in a large pot and cover them with water. Add the onion, celery ribs, carrot chunks, salt, and pepper. Bring to a boil and then reduce heat, cover, and simmer for 1½ hours.

Remove from heat. Take out the chicken breasts to cool enough to handle. Discard the onion, celery ribs, and carrot chunks from the stock. When cool enough, discard the skin and bones from the chicken. Chop the chicken into bite-sized pieces.

Bring the seasoned broth back to a boil and add the uncooked pasta. Gently boil for 5 minutes. Add the sliced celery, sliced carrots, and cooked chicken. Simmer until the pasta and vegetables are al dente. Stir in the heavy cream and butter. Season with additional salt and pepper if desired.

Notes

Chicken, Sausage, and Wild Rice Casserole

SERVES 6 | PREP 40 minutes |
COOK 1 hour for chicken then ½ hour for casserole

Ingredients

3 chicken breasts (or 2 large)

Salt and pepper, to taste

1 (6-ounce) package long grain and wild rice mix

2 cups chicken broth

½ pound hot bulk sausage

2 large white or yellow onions, chopped

2 (10.5-ounce) cans cream of mushroom soup

2 cups fresh crumbled bread

Directions

Place the chicken breasts in a large Dutch oven. Season generously with salt and pepper. Cover with water and cook until tender, approximately 60 to 90 minutes. Remove the chicken and save the broth. This can be done ahead of time. Dice the chicken and set aside.

Cook the wild rice according to package directions substituting some of the reserved broth for water.

Brown the sausage and chopped onion. Drain to remove excess grease. Add the mushroom soup to the sausage mixture.

Spread the rice in a 9 x 13-inch casserole dish. Top with diced chicken. Spread the sausage and mushroom soup over the chicken. Cover with bread crumbs. Cover with foil.

When ready to serve, bake at 375 degrees covered with the foil for 30 minutes or until hot. Remove foil and bake 5 minutes more to brown.

Notes

White Bean and Spinach Soup

SERVES 6 | PREP 30 minutes (after soaking beans overnight) | COOK 1 hour

Ingredients

1 cup dried Great Northern beans

3 tablespoons extra-virgin olive oil

¾ cup white or yellow onions, chopped

½ cup carrots, sliced

1½ cups chopped fresh baby spinach

5 cups chicken broth

1 teaspoon garlic, chopped

1 bay leaf

Salt and pepper, to taste

3 tablespoons parsley, chopped

Grated Parmesan cheese for garnish

Directions

Place the beans in a large container and generously cover with water. Soak overnight. Drain the beans, reserving up 2 cups of liquid.

In a large Dutch oven, heat the oil. Sauté the onions and carrots in the oil until tender. Add the spinach and cook, stirring, until wilted. Add the chicken broth, bean water, beans, garlic, and bay leaf. Partially cover and simmer for 1 hour. Remove the bay leaf. Puree half the soup in a blender or food processor. Return to the pot of remaining soup and mix well. Season with salt and pepper. Stir in the parsley.

Serve with Parmesan cheese.

Notes

Macaroni Beef Supper

SERVES 6 | PREP 30 minutes | COOK 25 minutes

Ingredients

1 (8-ounce) box macaroni, cooked and drained

1½ cups American cheese

1 pound ground beef

1 medium white or yellow onion, chopped

1 green pepper, chopped

1 (15½-ounce) jar spaghetti sauce with mushrooms

1 (8-ounce) can tomato sauce

½ teaspoon salt

½ teaspoon black pepper

1 clove garlic, minced

1 (6-ounce) package mozzarella cheese

Directions

Toss hot macaroni with the American cheese and set aside.

Brown ground beef in a large skillet. Stir in onion and green pepper. Add the spaghetti sauce, tomato sauce, and salt. Add black pepper and garlic to the beef mixture and simmer for 15 minutes. If it becomes to dry, add a little water.

In a 2-quart casserole dish, layer half of the macaroni and cheese, half of the meat sauce, and half of the mozzarella cheese. Repeat the layers.

Bake at 375 degrees for 20 to 25 minutes or until hot throughout.

Notes

This yummy entree can be prepared ahead of time and baked at serving time.

Mississippi Corn Bread

SERVES 6 | PREP 20 minutes | COOK 40 minutes

Ingredients

1 cup self-rising flour

1 cup sour cream

2 eggs, slightly beaten

½ cup vegetable oil

½ cup cream-style corn

1 medium white or yellow onion, chopped

Directions

Stir the flour, sour cream, eggs, oil, corn, and onion in a large bowl to mix. Pour into a greased 8-inch-square baking dish or 9-inch iron skillet.

Bake at 400 degrees for 40 minutes or until golden brown.

Notes

Easy Lemonade Cake

SERVES 12 to 20 | PREP 30 minutes | COOK 40 minutes

Ingredients

1 box lemon supreme cake mix

1 (3¾-ounce) package instant lemon pudding

4 eggs

1 cup plus 2 tablespoons water

½ cup butter, melted

Topping:

1 (6-ounce) can frozen lemonade, thawed

1 (16-ounce) box or bag confectioners' sugar

Directions

Grease and flour a 9 x 13-inch cake pan. In a large bowl, beat the cake mix, instant pudding, eggs, water, and butter until smooth and creamy. Pour the batter in the prepared pan. Bake for 35 minutes at 350 degrees.

While the cake is baking, prepare the topping by stirring together the thawed lemonade and powdered sugar.

As soon as the cake comes out of the oven, cut it into squares (without removing it from the pan) and pour the topping over the hot cake. Bake 5 more minutes.

Notes

Lobster Rolls

SERVES 6 | PREP 20 minutes | COOK 2 minutes

Ingredients

1 pound cooked lobster chunks, fresh or frozen

½ cup mayonnaise

¼ cup celery, finely chopped

2 teaspoons lemon juice

Two dashes hot pepper sauce

¼ teaspoon salt

¼ teaspoon pepper

2 teaspoons chives, chopped

6 split-top hot dog rolls

2 tablespoons butter, melted

Directions

Cut the lobster chunks into smaller pieces but still keep them chunky. Place in a large bowl.

In a smaller bowl, combine the mayonnaise, celery, lemon juice, hot pepper sauce, salt, pepper, and chives. Add mixture to the lobster and stir well.

Preheat the oven to 400 degrees. Brush the hot dog rolls with butter. Lightly toast rolls in the oven for 2 minutes or until lightly browned.

Fill each roll with lobster salad.

Notes

New England Clam Chowder

SERVES 6 | PREP 25 minutes | COOK 30 minutes

Ingredients

6 tablespoons butter

1 large white or yellow onion, chopped

2 small carrots, chopped

1 baking potato, peeled and diced

½ cup all-purpose flour

1 pint shucked clams with liquid

3 (8-ounce) jars clam juice

1 cup heavy cream

1 cup half-and-half

Salt and pepper, to taste

1 teaspoon fresh dill weed, chopped

Directions

Melt the butter in a large Dutch oven. Add the onions, carrots, and potato and sauté for a few minutes until the vegetables are tender. Lower heat, stir in flour, and cook, stirring frequently, until smooth and lightly browned. Set aside to cool.

In a separate pot, combine the clams, their liquid, and the clam juice. Bring to a boil, then lower heat and simmer for about 15 minutes.

Very gradually pour the hot clams and juice into the Dutch oven with the flour mixture, stirring constantly, and bring to a boil. Then reduce heat. Stir in the cream, half-and-half, salt, pepper, and fresh dill weed.

Notes

Cranberry Pecan Cornbread

SERVES 8 | PREP 30 minutes | COOK 30 minutes

Ingredients

1 cup sweetened dried cranberries

1 tablespoon orange peel, freshly grated

Juice of 2 to 3 large oranges (about ½ cup)

1 cup all-purpose flour

1 cup cornmeal

2 teaspoons baking powder

1¼ teaspoons salt

½ teaspoon baking soda

3 large eggs

1½ cups sour cream

½ cup maple syrup

6 tablespoons butter, melted

½ cup toasted pecans

Directions

Combine the cranberries, orange peel, and orange juice. Let stand for 30 minutes, then drain.

Generously grease a springform pan and wrap foil around the outside to make sure the batter doesn't leak into your oven.

Combine the flour, cornmeal, baking powder, salt, and baking soda in a large bowl.

In another bowl, whisk together the eggs, sour cream, syrup, and melted butter. Add this to the dry ingredients and stir just until blended. Mix in the cranberries and toasted pecans. Pour the batter into the prepared pan.

Bake at 400 degrees for about 30 minutes or until done.

Notes

The toasted pecans, cranberries, orange juice, and grated orange peel make this a great choice for the holidays, but I enjoy it any time of year. Served on the side, it turns a simple soup into a special meal. Try it with the Clam Chowder or White Bean and Spinach Soup.

You are special today
You are special today

The Best Brownies EVER

SERVES 16 to 20 | PREP 20 minutes | COOK 25 minutes

Ingredients

4 eggs, beaten

2 cups sugar

2 cups all-purpose flour

1 tablespoon vanilla extract

1 cup butter

4 ounces unsweetened chocolate

Frosting:

½ cup (1 stick) butter

4 tablespoons unsweetened cocoa powder

6 tablespoons whole milk

1 teaspoon vanilla extract

1 (16-ounce) box or bag confectioners' sugar

2 cups mini marshmallows (optional)

Directions

Beat together the eggs and sugar in a large mixing bowl. Mix in the flour and vanilla extract.

Melt the butter and chocolate together in a heavy saucepan or the microwave, stirring to blend. Add to the batter and mix well.

Spread into a greased 9 x 13-inch pan. Bake at 350 degrees for 25 minutes. Be careful not to overcook. Check after about 22 minutes.

Prepare the frosting while the brownies are baking.

Add the butter, cocoa, and milk to a saucepan and bring to a boil. Boil gently, stirring constantly, for 1 minute. Remove from heat and stir in vanilla extract. Gradually stir in confectioners' sugar. Fold the marshmallows into the warm frosting and spread the frosting over the brownies.

Notes

Goody Bars

MAKES 2 dozen squares | PREP 30 minutes | COOK 45 minutes

Ingredients

1 box white cake mix

½ cup butter, melted

3 eggs

¾ cup pecans, chopped

1 (8-ounce) package cream cheese, softened

1 (16-ounce) box or bag confectioners' sugar

Directions

Stir together the cake mix, melted butter, and 1 egg. Grease and flour a 9 x 13-inch pan. Spread batter over the bottom of the prepared pan.

Sprinkle the pecans evenly over the batter.

Beat the cream cheese, powdered sugar, and 2 more eggs until smooth and creamy. Spread on top of the pecans.

Bake at 350 degrees for 45 minutes. Cut into 2-inch squares to serve.

Notes

Favorite Frosted Sugar Cookies

MAKES 2 dozen cookies | PREP 1 hour | COOK 10 minutes

Ingredients

1 cup (2 sticks) butter, softened

2 cups sugar

3 eggs

2 teaspoons vanilla extract

4 cups pre-sifted, all-purpose flour

2 teaspoons baking powder

Frosting:

½ cup (1 stick) butter, softened

5 cups confectioners' sugar

⅓ cup milk

2 teaspoons vanilla extract

Food coloring (optional)

Directions

Beat the butter and sugar with an electric mixer until fluffy. Add eggs one at a time, beating after each. Stir in the vanilla extract, flour, and baking powder. Mix well. Refrigerate until firm enough to roll out (about 1 hour).

On a well-floured surface, roll out the dough ⅛-inch thick. Cut with cookie cutters. Place on a baking sheet and bake at 325 degrees for 10 minutes until light brown.

While the cookies are cooling, prepare the frosting. Beat the butter and sugar until creamy. Mix in the milk and vanilla one tablespoon at a time until the frosting reaches a spreadable consistency. Use food colors, if desired.

Notes

Screen Time

As unexpected as a career in television was in my early years, when the opportunity knocked, I answered. And what a joy it has been.

Reflections

The Audition 84
The Adventure Begins.......86
Behind the Scenes...........92
New Beginnings..............96
So Many Interesting People..98
Leaving WBTV 107

The Audition

WBTV had replaced *The Betty Feezor Show* with a magazine-style show called *Top O' the Day*. Miraculously on that day when my mother told me to call the station, Anna Rufty, the kind woman in personnel, agreed to have me come in for an interview to discuss how I might contribute to the new show. My answer to everything asked during the interview was, "Yes, I can do that," optimistically and confidently thinking that I could and would learn.

I learned later that after talking with me that day, Anna called the producer of the new show, Cathy Painter, saying that she had someone she wanted Cathy to meet. Cathy asked Anna how many years I had been in television and the size of the market where I had been working. Anna confessed that I had zero television experience, that I was just a Charlotte-based mom who could cook. Cathy was shocked and exclaimed, "I do not have time to talk with someone who walks in off the street with no experience." Anna did not give up and convinced Cathy to give me a chance saying, "I really think you should meet this one." Cathy and I met, and strangely enough, she arranged for me to do an audition.

I will never forget the day I was ushered into the bright lights of a television studio in the biggest, oldest, most-watched TV station in the Carolinas and one of the oldest, most-respected stations in the country. This station pioneered taping and broadcasting in color. It was among the first to broadcast live TV news and then national network news.

Cathy, the beautiful, polished, professional producer, introduced me to the director and cameramen who

would tape my audition. This should have felt like a life-changing dream come true, but suddenly it felt like a nightmare. *I was terrified. What was I thinking?* I had never been in front of multiple cameras, had no idea where to look or how to take time cues from the floor manager or the director or how to deal with a microphone. I had never had a class, instruction, or experience with television. I just liked to watch it.

I got through the audition, but I was awful. I expressed my gratitude for the opportunity and hurried home, never telling *anyone* (except my mom) that I had done such a bold, crazy thing. I assumed no one would ever know what I had done since I was certain I would never hear from WBTV again. I was sure they were probably still laughing and wondering how I got in the building and convinced someone to give me an audition. I was so embarrassed that for six weeks I wouldn't even watch TV.

Suddenly, out of the blue six weeks later, a letter from WBTV came in the mail. Staring at the envelope, I could not imagine why they were contacting me other than possibly to tell me never call them again. To my shock, the letter was so upbeat and kind, saying that it was clear I had much to learn, but they believed there was potential. They asked me to come back and try again. I was surprised at how excited and eager I was, completely forgetting my earlier shame and embarrassment.

I went back again to do a segment ... and again ... and again until I got the job as cohost. C.J. Underwood, my TV cohost of *Top o' the Day* for years once told me, "Talent ain't nothing but wanting to do something bad enough." This is another example in my life when I knew God winked and did something for me that seemed impossible, and I did my best to do my part.

The Adventure Begins

When I began my job, I was fully aware that Betty Feezor was beloved, and I feared I would never be accepted in her noon-time slot. Even though I was very experienced with food and crafts, I did not have a degree in home economics like Betty did. I thought all the viewers would want to know what credentials gave me the right to share recipes.

To solve that issue, I applied and was accepted at L'Acadamie de Cuisine, a well-respected chef school near Washington, DC. Every Monday for many months, I would get up at 2:00 a.m. and fly to DC (having taped my segments for that day during the previous week). Francois Dionot, the acclaimed chef, liked my story so much that he taught me privately from 9:00 a.m. to 9:00 p.m. on his day off. I then caught a plane back to Charlotte and continued with my TV work live the rest of the week. I was doing all this with a two-year-old at home and a baby on the way, but I was determined to earn the audience's approval.

It was not easy and—I later learned—was unnecessary. The kind, wonderful audience never once asked about my training or education. My diploma never

A New Star at WBTV

BARBARA STUTTS-
SHE'S A 'NATURAL'

made it out of a drawer. The people in my TV audience were accepting, loving, welcoming, and kind. I loved every second of sharing my day with these wonderful people. I loved seeing and hearing from them and still do after all these years. My favorite comments are from young adults who tell me that their grandmothers never missed my show, and as children, they were not allowed to speak while I was giving out ingredients and instructions.

I was also in awe of the people who worked at WBTV. I had grown up watching them—Clyde McLean, Jim Patterson, Fred Kirby. I shared an office with Jim Patterson—Uncle Jim. He had

I was also in awe of the people who worked at WBTV. I had grown up watching them—Clyde McLean, Jim Patterson, Fred Kirby.

signed the tummy of my stuffed animal called an "autograph hound" when I stood in line at the Rogers Theater to meet him as a child. I could hardly believe that I was learning from the best—true pioneers of television. They seemed even more talented off screen, these fantastic, multitalented performers, speakers, and for me, amazing teachers and mentors.

How grateful I was and always will be for the opportunity to "learn by doing" from the best in the business.

Almost everything was *live*, so my mistakes were broadcast for all to see—the time cake splattered all over my face, *twice* when I set the kitchen counter on fire, and many other nightmarish things. Understanding people behind the scenes, John Hutchinson, Jim Babb, Cullie Tarleton, John Edgerton, and Ty Boyd, generously guided me and gave me a chance to learn and grow. They created so many opportunities for me. Marion Meginnis and Mark DeCastrique were so patient and kind as they worked to teach me TV skills to handle the opportunities. John Carter, from my home county, arrived about the same time I did but was much more prepared for a job on TV. He cheered me on from the start and still does. Other talented broadcast journalists like Lori Thomas and Paul Cameron were cheerleaders for this girl with no broadcast training.

I wanted every person working for or watching WBTV to know that I *never* considered myself "taking Betty Feezor's place." That was impossible. I was adamant about correcting anyone who used that phrase to introduce me. She was a legend. I was especially

I loved every second of sharing my day with these wonderful people. I loved seeing and hearing from them and still do after all these years.

concerned about how her husband and children would feel toward me. I did not need to be worried because they were also extraordinary. They welcomed me and made me feel like a family member. I am smiling as I write this just thinking about how they treated me as if I were one of Betty's children, like another sibling. We shared so many wonderful times together.

When Betty's husband, Turner, died, Lynn Feezor presented me with a photo album filled with pictures of us through the years, just as she had done for all of Betty's children. John, Lynn, Betty Cole, Robert, and I remain friends—and family.

Another legendary broadcaster who influenced my journey in a big way was Ty Boyd, the "voice of the Carolinas." As his talent became known globally and his reputation as a motivational speaker took him around the world, he had to give up some things at WBTV, including his advertising spokesperson role for large businesses in the Carolinas. He generously suggested that I take his place for some of those important accounts. Besides blessing me with these opportunities, he prepared and motivated me as only Ty Boyd could. I was grateful just to know him. He would come to my early TV and radio commercial shoots and coach me. My gratitude for how he helped my career is enormous. Ty has gone to heaven, but his wonderful family and I remain friends.

Because of Ty, I became the spokesperson for Harris Teeter grocery stores. This was a career changer. I loved every day of representing them. It was a pleasure to do their commercials and appear in their stores where my recipes and cookbooks could be found. They sponsored many special events for me. This made me visible on all local TV stations at all times of the day and night, not just at noon. I had the joy of being their spokesperson for twelve happy years.

One Monday morning before my show, I was called into the WBTV advertising director's office where I was told that in one week, I would no longer be working for Harris Teeter and would become the spokesperson for Winn Dixie. I was shocked speechless (unusual for me), but this was the beginning of learning more about the business side of TV. My naïveté and fierce loyalty for Harris Teeter led me to say, "I cannot do that. What will the people watching, not to mention my dear friends at Harris Teeter, think?!" I quickly became aware that money talks, and I had to listen. Winn Dixie had offered a whole lot of money for me, not to me directly but to the station that employed me.

My protests did not go unheard, however. The advertising department agreed to let Harris Teeter know about the change and offered them the chance to match the number. If they did, I could stay with Harris Teeter. Harris Teeter executives called me to express their appreciation but also to say that they were much smaller than Winn Dixie and could not afford to match the price. They assured me there were no hard feelings. It was business.

OK, that's good, I supposed, but what was Winn Dixie going to say knowing I tried to get out of their deal? I was worried but did not need to be. The next day, the wonderful Winn Dixie executives called me in and said, "Barbara, we hope you will be as loyal to us as you were to Harris Teeter. We admire that." Whew. This turned out to be another enormous opportunity for me, emphasizing again to always just do the right thing.

Winn Dixie had one of the most talented, thoughtful, brilliant management teams who took me under their wing and continued my TV and advertising education. Because of them, I got to do TV shows, commercials, and videos, not just locally, but also regionally and nationally. They introduced me to their food companies and their marketing agencies, which later led to shows, commercials, and media tours for the biggest names in corporate America. They created a show just for me called *Close to Home*, which I joyfully did for many years with the delightful Anne Oberlander. To this day, I only represent the companies and the people that I believe in, but Winn Dixie is the company that opened that window of opportunity, allowing me to choose the products and services that I most admired.

Those recipes from my early TV days are still enjoyed today with a little tweaking. At Thanksgiving, I receive many messages from all over the country asking for recipes that people loved and enjoyed growing up in the Charlotte area.

'Miss Wonderful'

Prestigious Home Service Insurance Company

Barbara Stutts To Host Her Own Show, "Barbara," Beginning April 26 On WBTV

CHARLOTTE, N.C.-Barbara Stutts, a favorite of viewers of WBTV's "Top O' The Day," will become host of her own show, entitled "Barbara," beginning Monday, April 26th on WBTV, Channel 3. The half-hour program, to be seen weekdays at 1:00 pm, will be produced by Jefferson Productions and will also air o[n] WBTV's sister station, WWBT in Richmond, Virgini[a] at 11:30 am weekdays.

"Barbara" will be different in style and substan[ce] from the variety format of "Top O' The Day." It will [be] taped before an invited live audience. Guest expe[rts] will join Barbara to discuss a single subject per sh[ow] that is of particular interest to women. The audie[nce] will participate in the show by asking questions [and] making comments on the topic of the day - which m[ay] be anything from dealing with children to how to [...] in today's complex world. Barbara will also pres[ent a] short cooking feature each day.

In the few, short years that Barbara Stutts ha[s been] seen on WBTV, she has become one of the st[ation's] most popular personalities. In addition to her [...] and crafting talents, Barbara has proved hers[elf] an expert in a variety of areas from intervi[...]

The Jeffcaster

A Newsletter Published Weekly for the Employees of Jefferson-Pilot Broadcasting and Their Families

VOLUME XVI, NUMBER 29 — CHARLOTTE, NC — SEPTEMBER 5, 1983

Insurance Costs Being Watched

BOB — BARBARA

Bob and Barbara To Appear On Nationally Syndicated Shows

I was shocked speechless (unusual for me), but this was the beginning of learning more about the business side of TV.

Behind the Scenes

Whatever your job, I suggest going above and beyond what is expected to reap the most benefits from your career. Early on, I volunteered for everything. I was willing to sweep the floor or be on all-night telethons. My small-town work ethic made that easy for me. My reputation for working tirelessly, and with gratitude for the chance, brought more opportunities. I continued to learn from everyone on camera and off.

To give you an idea of the talent behind the scenes at WBTV, one of my commercial producers has now become one of the most well-known, beloved radio hosts in the country–Sheri Lynch. Her show, *Bob & Sheri*, is syndicated in markets around the world, and she donates her valuable time to many philanthropic organizations. She began at WBTV producing commercials, and I was fortunate and blessed that she produced mine.

Can you imagine how much fun it was to be on a commercial shoot with Sheri Lynch? She was close friends with Anne Oberlander, the producer of one of my TV shows, and would also visit us on that set. Having these two brilliant and funny writers and producers together made it challenging to keep from cracking up during some very serious on-camera moments, but no matter what I did, their brilliant production skills made everything look perfect.

After a few years of appearing on *Top O' the Day* and all sorts of specials and telethons, I finally began to learn more about how to do TV. I had some difficulty learning while appearing live. All kinds of crazy moments that make me cringe took place. Many may remember the cake batter flying out of the mixer onto my face, since they replay that at every WBTV anniversary show, and there were also a couple of kitchen fires captured on live TV. I also had some embarrassing interviews that made me worry I would not be back the next day. One that comes to mind is when I was interviewing a well-known male heart throb of daytime TV. We were sitting on a sofa with a live audience at *The Southern Women's Show* when suddenly he just leapt over on top of me and began kissing me as if I was appearing on his soap opera. The audience gasped. My very young son was visiting the show that day and was horrified at the sight. I later learned that the star was dared to do it, and he had nothing to lose. He flew back to New York that day. I recovered and was grateful I still had a job the next day.

As my TV experience grew, the wonderful people mentoring me gave me new opportunities. C.J. and I had a blast. I hope our TV friends watching enjoyed each day as much as we did. C.J. was like a brother to me.

Along with our daily show, we went on assignments all over the world, literally taking viewers along with us on trips and cruises, taping the stories during the day and hosting our guests for dinner in the evenings. On those trips, I was blessed to do extraordinary stories. I flew in a helicopter over an erupting volcano and tried to sound calm. In Alaska, I reported from a bitterly cold glacier straddling a huge crack in the ice. I stood in a field in Holland with tulips as far as the eye could see. I showed our audience how diamonds were cut in Belgium, the diamond capitol of the world. There were many more

special, exciting moments all over the world that I treasure and will never forget for a second how blessed and fortunate I was.

One of my most memorable moments of all was in Paris when the designer famous for dressing Audrey Hepburn and other iconic stars sent a car for me to tour his new perfumery just outside the city. Hubert deGivenchy will be special to me forever. I still wear the perfume he was creating that day. He gave me gallons of it to bring home. *Ysatis* has been my "signature fragrance" since 1984. That trip to Paris intensified my passion for fashion. We had amazing adventures on those trips and I still enjoy hearing from the great people who traveled with us.

Top O' the Day was broadcast Monday through Friday from noon to 1 p.m. Preparing for the cooking segment and several interviews each day was demanding and time consuming, but I loved my job. I was especially grateful that I was allowed to prepare for the show at home so that I could see my children off to school and be there soon after they returned. After they went to bed, I stayed up late to finish preparing for the next day.

New opportunities continued to come my way as I gained more experience. I began doing a very early show called *Good Morning* with Jim Patterson and Bob Taylor, then ran home to see my children off to school before heading back to the station to tape segments and then cohost the live portions of *Top O' the Day* at noon. Early afternoons were spent taping additional shows like *Living in the Carolinas, Close to Home, Racing Home,* segments for *PM Magazine,* and later, a two-hour radio show. I sometimes had to go back at night to tape other projects like my show *Barbara.*

I also produced five cookbooks and promoted those with appearances at Harris Teeter and later, Winn Dixie stores throughout the market.

Then there were the commercials, which I especially enjoyed. I did hundreds of commercials for companies whose services and products I loved and admired—for grocery stores, furniture stores, home improvement stores, Auto Bell, and many more. Plaza Appliance was a favorite. Owners Bill, Bill Jr., and Kim Pleasants, remain very close friends today. There were more TV and radio projects that kept me busy, but you get the idea. I loved my job and worked very hard at it.

As many of you know, and others can guess, while Clyde and I both loved our jobs and each other, our busy careers were not healthy for our marriage. We were both enjoying our work and coworkers who understood because they were in similar situations. This is not an excuse, just the truth.

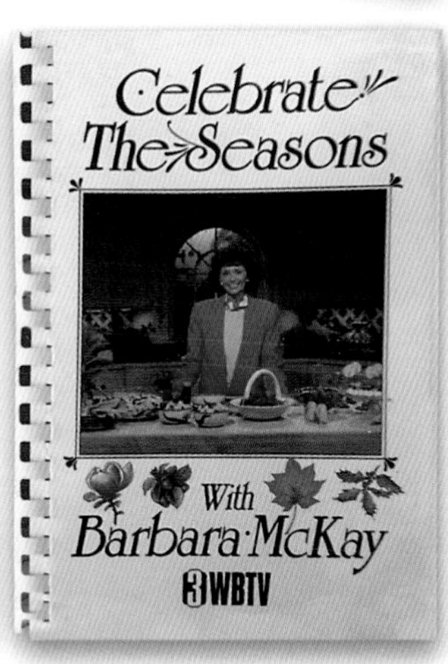

New Beginnings

Life was hectic. Busy careers and the many distractions that accompany them could put a strain on any marriage, especially when that marriage begins long before the individuals are all grown up and understand themselves better.

I never imagined being divorced. While divorce is not what God wants for us, forgiveness, grace, and redemption are very much a part of His plan and a way of drawing us closer. This girl of strong character and faith headed into some uncharted territory in adulthood, which taught me, among many other lessons, never to say never and especially never to judge others. Until we are in specific situations with unique circumstances, we cannot be sure how we would respond.

Many of you know the agony of the divorce process. It is an intensely painful and trying time. It represents

the loss of dreams and commitments and compromises our beliefs. It brings on disappointment, stress, confusion, and grief. It is especially painful when it involves people in the public eye. Mine brought harsh judgment and hateful comments from people who had never met me or had no clue of the actual circumstances. They preferred to believe sensationalized, silly, laughable rumors because the truth was boring. Thankfully, the majority of people were compassionate, understanding, and comforting. I needed those people.

I won't go into the personal details or describe what it's like to go through an emotional wringer and still stay perky on TV every day. I will skip to something more important, which is that within a year, all four of us had remarried and moved on with a renewed sense of love, hope, and optimism. I married coworker Mike McKay. He and I have been happily married for thirty-four years.

While my first marriage went away, the love and respect remain to this day. I enjoy spending time with Clyde's sisters, Carol and Beth. We still consider ourselves family. My children with Clyde and his children with Michele enjoy fun times together. They, their mom, and I have fun at Carolina Panthers games. These resilient, loving, respectful relationships may be a disappointment to those who did not wish us all well, but as Clyde said to me as the two of us spent time together just before he went to heaven, all that matters is *love*.

Photo By: Paul Williams Photograph

I will skip to something more important, which is that within a year, all four of us had remarried and moved on with a renewed sense of love, hope, and optimism. I married coworker Mike McKay. He and I have been happily married for thirty-four years.

So Many Interesting People

As my role grew at WBTV, I got to meet many famous and fascinating people. Mike and I both did movie junkets traveling to cities around the world to meet the people who make movies happen—star, producers, directors, writers. These usually took place in New York or Los Angeles but often at the locations where the movies were made. We interviewed the movie makers and produced reviews of the movies with interviews and clips to air on various WBTV shows. It was fun. We did this at least twice a month for about twenty years. I am often asked who I enjoyed interviewing most. While I had the fun of meeting, spending time with, and talking with many movie and TV stars, my most treasured moments were with fashion designers. More on that later.

Because of my work with the movie industry and my TV shows, I got to meet many people in the entertainment industry. I wish I had photos with them all. Smartphones weren't around at the time for selfies, and I didn't want to impose on them by carrying in my Kodak and asking them to pose and someone to shoot. Even though I don't have the photos, the images and memories live forever in

my mind. I have already mentioned some of my favorite big stars earlier in the book, and here are just a few more recollections of so many special moments and people.

My Most Embarrassing Moment

I will start here and just get it out of the way. Here is the short version. My son, Michael, and I were attending a Hornets game. We were running a little late and arrived just after the national anthem.

The man sitting next to me and I struck up a friendly conversation. He was such a kind, caring gentleman and brought me M&Ms and a coke from the concessions. I found it so interesting when he told me he was from Tennessee. This was a Tuesday night. Why would someone come all the way from Tennessee on a weeknight to watch the Hornets? I asked and he told me that he sang the national anthem for the game. I was duly impressed, saying that I knew what a difficult song that is to perform and that he must be a good singer.

I was clueless. He told me that he liked to sing and perform. I still cringe all these years later as I say what happened next.

I told him that I hosted a local daytime TV show, and if it would be helpful to him, maybe he could come perform. After that came out of my mouth, I spotted some close friends sitting courtside. I told my singer-seatmate that I was going to pop down and visit some friends for a moment and asked if he would hold my big heavy coat and handbag. He so kindly obliged.

Michael and I ended up staying the rest of the game with the friends.

After it was over and we had remained chatting, it dawned on me that I never went back for my coat and bag. I exclaimed, "Oh my. I left my things with a stranger. Wonder what he did with them since he must have left to drive back to Tennessee!" I looked up at all the vacated seats, and there stood the nice man waiting for me to gather my things. I thanked him profusely and yet again invited him to be on my local show.

A week later I was watching TV and the *Country Music Awards* came on hosted by none other than my singer-seatmate—Vince Gill! The color drained from my face. I was mortified that I was sitting next to one of the most legendary, country music stars of *all time*, and I offered him a job. Vince Gill will always be my favorite country music singer, and he is as nice, wonderful, and even more humble and kind than he seems. *I am so sorry, Vince.* I will never get over it.

A Favorite Local Hero

I was so fortunate that during my time on TV, the press was very kind and supportive. They liked good news. I have happy memories of my time spent with many talented legends at the *Charlotte Observer* who were kind and generous with their comments, including Lew Powell, Helen Moore, Emery Wister, Olivia Fortson, and Kays Gary. The award-winning Kays was beloved by everyone who read the *Charlotte Observer*. His column was the most popular in the paper. He appeared on our noon TV show and later wrote about his experience. His column is one of my all-time favorites because he had known me since I was a baby. He wrote that all he could think about, as he was sitting beside me on TV, was remembering me as a drooling, babbling baby while he and my daddy watched the Washington Redskins on a great new invention called TV.

Glib, Talented, Successful and So Very Nice

Bruce Willis is fantastic. Before I met him the first time, his sharp wit made me think he might be difficult. I was very wrong about that. He is one of the most down-to-earth and kindest in the business. Interviewing him was always so special and fun. After interviewing him a couple of times, Mike and I were in New York for his latest movie. But it was *sale time* at Bergdorf's, and I wanted to be there when the doors opened. So I asked

Mike to do the interview without me. Very soon the phone rang, and I was told that Bruce would like for me to participate in the interview first, and then I could go shop. Whatever Bruce Willis wanted ... I was honored.

The Comedians

I loved every moment of the many, many comedians whom I interviewed, not just because I love to spend time with people who make me laugh, but also because so many are such kind, thoughtful, sincere people. Seeing the gentle, serious, and in some cases shy sides of them really endeared them to me even more. Here are a few of many with whom I had the joy to spend time.

Jerry Seinfeld came to the studio early and stayed late to appear on my noon time show, even though his segment was just five minutes. It was before he was super famous, but he sure was super funny, especially during the commercials. I had to stifle laughter throughout as he added comments on the other side of the camera as I cooked and did the rest of the show.

Steve Martin is a soft-spoken, kind, almost shy gentleman, not the wild and crazy one he plays. But as I was leaving, he handed me a note that makes me laugh every time I think of it all these years later. I still have it, but he would not want me to share it. I respect that.

Robin Williams was exactly what you would expect—full-on funny *all* the time. He is the only person I ever interviewed that I only had to ask him one question, and he would take it from there, creating a hilarious monologue that stopped only when the timer declared, "Time is up." But he still had a thoughtful, pensive side too. He said that when he was first beginning his career, he had a gig scheduled in Charlotte at a comedy club. *Three* people showed up, but he did his show as if it was standing room only, which I can totally believe since he always performed shows for me even though I was the only person in the room.

David Letterman is another kind, mannerly, thoughtful gentleman. He is the only star I interviewed who mailed a thank you note to me later.

Tim Conway—what a legend. He came to our studio, and as we chatted for a couple of hours, he never stopped "performing" and genuinely loved making me laugh. I'm so thankful I got to meet him and so sorry that I never got to meet Carol Burnett, one of my all-time favorites.

John Candy was an especially thoughtful, soft-spoken gentleman. My daughter, Elizabeth, went to Los Angeles with me for the interview, and I will always remember how kind he was to my daughter. He really was an Uncle Buck.

I am still enjoying Lily Tomlin on *Grace and Frankie*. I was afraid I would be intimated, but she was as friendly as she seems on screen. She seems like someone who would be a friend of mine if we lived in the same community. Speaking of her new show on Netflix, I went to a movie in Atlanta with "Grace" (Jane Fonda) and her husband at the time, Ted Turner. She is gorgeous.

There were many more including Tom Poston, Ted Danson, the casts of *Designing Women*, *Golden Girls*, *Murphy Brown*, *Dukes of Hazzard*, and other CBS shows since WBTV is a CBS affiliate.

Another Legend

It was such a joy to spend hours with Andy Griffith. He seemed like someone who would have been a friend of my daddy's. He came to the studio, and we talked for hours about Shelby (my hometown), Mount Airy (his hometown), and Mayberry. It was surreal. We had much in common.

Music Legends and More

It's still so amazing how I met Elvis as a child and completely embarrassed myself with Vince Gill as an adult. Years later, I met Michael Jackson at the Grammy Awards. It was very brief and hard to describe the look of a kind of sadness and innocence in the superstar's eyes. He was very nice, soft-spoken, and kind.

One of the nicest and most thoughtful music legends I ever met is Jon Bon Jovi. I interviewed him for the movie *Young Guns,* which inspired his *Blaze of Glory* album. I told him that my son was a huge fan. Later that day, he searched for and found me in the hotel and gave me signed memorabilia to give to Michael. Such a nice man.

Speaking of the movie *Young Guns,* that weekend I also interviewed Lou Diamond Phillips, Charlie Sheen, Terry O'Quinn, Jack Palance, and Kiefer Sutherland. Very early on the morning of the interviews, I went down to breakfast in the hotel. There were only two other people there at 6:00 a.m.—Kiefer and his girlfriend. I didn't recognize her face but sure did her voice. She was talking about her work for the day and already had her hair and makeup done, ready to film. I had only seen her in *Steel Magnolias,* and on this day, she looked very different. She was ready for her scene in *Pretty Woman* wearing the red dress. It was Julia Roberts.

A Few More Superstars

When I was in New York interviewing Harrison Ford for *Patriot Games*, the power went out. I had to sit in the dark for much of the morning with Harrison Ford. Oh, poor me. He is so normal and down-to-earth.

I interviewed William Petersen for *Young Guns II* early one morning in Los Angeles. Right after the interview, I received a call in my hotel room. William said that his fifteen-year-old daughter was with him and asked if I would mind if she tagged along with me the rest of the day since he was very busy. I said that I had interviews to do. He said she wants my job one day. Of course, I said yes, and we had a fun day together.

I met Mel Gibson in Maine for his movie *The Man Without a Face*. Mel was very kind, but I will never forget his publicist. She frightened me. I asked a question, and from the sidelines, she shouted, "You can't ask him that!" It was a very mundane question about food. If he was paying her to be a bulldog, he was getting his money's worth.

I interviewed Kevin Costner first for *Silverado* when he was just beginning his career and then for two other movies after he was a giant star. He was always the same: charming, friendly, and a little flirty, which was innocent and fun.

The World of Racing

I've been blessed to know many of NASCAR's biggest stars from Junior Johnson to Jimmie Johnson and his wife, Chandra. I got to know that world through my special friends and neighbors, Rick and Linda Hendrick.

Many years ago, I wrote a cookbook with John Kilgo, a wonderful friend and broadcast legend. I was doing a TV show for Raycom, *Racing Home*, about the families of NASCAR. The book had stories about the racing legends and included the recipes for their favorite foods. I spent time rocking on the porch with Richard Petty. I played piano with Jeff Gordon at his home. I rode on the back of Geoff Bodine's motorcycle around the Charlotte Motor Speedway track. I met dozens of drivers. Two of my most memorable times were with two of the sport's biggest stars.

Books have been written, and movies have been made about Junior Johnson. He started it all. What a joy it was for my husband Mike and me to be invited to dinner in North Wilkesboro at the home of Junior and his lovely wife, Lisa. It was just the four of us, and it was mesmerizing to hear Junior tell the fascinating stories

of the beginning of NASCAR. I could have listened for many more hours. Their home was gorgeous with all sorts of racing treasures. One of my most favorite was seeing his framed pardon from President Ronald Reagan for a 1956 moonshining conviction. Junior recently passed away. Lisa and I remain friends.

I met Dale Earnhardt as we were both starting our careers many years ago. I went to his racing shop to interview him. I climbed in his car, and that was not easy since the doors do not open. It was a memorable and fun time. Many years later, I was at the track in the pit area one afternoon visiting other friends. I saw Dale from a distance. It had been a lot of years since we first met. I walked over to say hello and reintroduced myself, thinking he probably would not even remember our earlier time together since he had become a superstar and met people all over the world. He gave me a hug and scolded me with a smile, saying, "Barbara, I just got famous. I didn't lose my memory." The world lost a fine man when he went to heaven.

Leaving WBTV

I loved my dream job and never wanted to leave it, but change is inevitable. My cohost, C.J. Underwood, moved back to the news department, but we remained close friends until the day his life ended from colon cancer. My new cohost was one of the brightest and most talented people I have ever known. The brilliant, beloved Mike Collins became the new cohost of *Top O' the Day* with me.

Mike Collins continues to be one of the Queen City's most treasured, admired talents. He could have worked anywhere in the world. I am so thankful he chose Charlotte, North Carolina, and so is Charlotte. *Charlotte Talks*, his daily talk-radio show, is a must for all who want to be entertained and informed. Outside of radio, he writes, sings, dances, and plays musical instruments as well as he talks. He continues to be a dear friend. Starting my day with him five days a week for years was another huge blessing.

I loved my dream job and never wanted to leave it, but change is inevitable.

Being the good and protective friend that he was, Mike shared with me his thoughts that change may be coming to WBTV. Mike was intuitive and would have made a great investigative reporter. I listened, but it was my nature to just blissfully go through each day enjoying the moment. Therefore, Mike was far more prepared than I was when change came.

The station decided it was time to become all news. That was the new direction of local TV with all other programming coming from the networks. Budgets were streamlined, and instead of popular personalities, local stations wanted serious journalists and meteorologists who were also less expensive. While the station's management and I remained great friends, and my show never lost its highest ratings in the market, there just was not a place anymore for a perky TV personality who was not a news journalist.

This sudden change was magnified when my husband Mike's job was also terminated the same day. While research and ratings showed that he was the most-popular personality in the market, he was also the highest paid. The entire creative services department was dismantled, and everything was moved to news—without us. I went to work one morning filled with the usual excitement of what the day may bring and went home with no income, no job, and no idea of what was next.

I was deeply saddened that my daily TV show was over and very frightened as to what I could do to earn a living and make sure my children were not affected. But I was also filled with gratitude that I enjoyed such an amazing job with the most wonderful people for decades. It was miraculous that I ever had such an awesome opportunity. I will always feel enormous admiration and appreciation for WBTV and its people. Many of us from that era still have close ties and a very special bond.

This upheaval never for a second shook my Christian faith. It strengthened it. I praised God for the privilege of doing something I loved for decades, let Him know I was excited about whatever was coming next, and prayed that He would provide. He did.

Favorite Recipes from My Daily TV Years

I still laugh (and sometimes cringe) over memorable moments cooking on live TV. It certainly isn't a career for the faint-hearted. These recipes from those years are still staples in my kitchen at home.

Taco Pie 110
Seven-Layer Mexican Dip 111
Parmesan Cheese Puffs 112
Broccoli Bread 113
Lida's Cheese Biscuits 114
Hearty Vegetable Beef Soup 115
Creamy Broccoli Soup 116
Baked Potato Soup 117
Crunchy Asian Spinach Salad 119
Curried Turkey Twist 120
Beef Enchiladas 121
Ginger Orange Beef 123
John Boy and Billy's Chili 124
Sesame Chicken Tacos 125
Dijon Sherry Chicken 126
Calabash Cove Crab Au Gratin 127
Sauteed Scallops with Pea Pods and Water Chestnuts 128
Shrimp and Creamy Grits 129
La Strada Pasta Salad 130
Seafood Fettuccine 131
Sheri Lynch's Pasta with Fresh Tomatoes 132
Baked Vidalia Onions 133
Elvis Presley Pound Cake 135
Roasted Vegetables Parmesan 136
Cheerwine Cake 137
Killer Key Lime Pie 138

Taco Pie

SERVES 6 | PREP 20 minutes | COOK 25 minutes

Ingredients

Crust:

1 refrigerated 9-inch pie crust

½ cup corn chips, crushed

Filling:

1 pound ground beef

1 (1.2-ounce) package taco seasoning mix

½ cup water

⅓ cup black olives, sliced

1 cup sour cream

1 cup Cheddar cheese, grated

¼ cup crushed corn chips

Garnish:

Shredded lettuce

Chopped tomatoes

Chopped cilantro

Directions

Place the pie crust in a pie plate. Sprinkle with crushed corn chips.

Brown the ground beef. Stir in the seasoning mix, water, and olives. Spread the meat mixture into the crust. Spread with sour cream. Top with grated cheese. Bake at 375 degrees for 20 to 25 minutes. Garnish with lettuce, tomatoes, and cilantro to taste.

Notes

I prepared this recipe on TV on May 1, 1978, and I still enjoy it to this day. I later learned that my daddy made the business associate he was traveling with that day stop at an appliance store, so he could see my first TV appearance. I looked like a deer in headlights.

Seven-Layer Mexican Dip

SERVES 8 | PREP 15 minutes

Ingredients

1 (16-ounce) can refried beans

2 cups sour cream

1 (1.2-ounce) package taco seasoning mix

2 cups prepared guacamole

2 cups Cheddar cheese, shredded

4 green onions, diced

½ cup black olives, sliced

1 tomato, diced

Tortilla chips

Directions

Spread beans in the bottom of a 10-inch round, clear glass dish. Set aside.

Combine the sour cream and seasoning mix. Spread over the beans.

Spread guacamole over the sour cream mixture.

Sprinkle with cheese and top with onions, olives, and tomato.

Serve with tortilla chips.

Notes

This was the favorite of my daughter's friends. I remember seeing one friend accidentally drop the last bite on the floor. He just scraped it up and kept eating.

Parmesan Cheese Puffs

SERVES 30 | PREP 15 minutes | COOK 3 minutes

Ingredients

1 cup mayonnaise

¾ cup Parmesan cheese, grated

⅓ cup Vidalia onions, chopped

30 Ritz crackers

Directions

Heat broiler on low.

Stir mayonnaise, Parmesan, and onions together until well blended.

Spread onto crackers and place on a baking sheet.

Broil for 2 to 3 minutes or until the mayo mixture is bubbly and golden brown. Serve warm.

Notes

These make a quick and easy appetizer using ingredients you usually have on hand. The topping also makes a wonderful accompaniment to soups or salads when spread over a favorite bread and broiled.

Broccoli Bread

SERVES 6 | PREP 20 minutes | COOK 25 minutes

Ingredients

1 (10-ounce) package frozen broccoli

4 eggs, beaten

1 cup cottage cheese

1 teaspoon salt

1 medium white or yellow onion, chopped

½ cup (1 stick) butter, melted

1 (8.5-ounce) package cornmeal muffin mix

Directions

Cook broccoli as directed on the package and drain well.

In a large bowl, combine eggs, cottage cheese, salt, onion, butter, and cornmeal and mix well.

Spread into a baking dish and bake at 400 degrees for 25 minutes.

Notes

Lida's Cheese Biscuits

MAKES 2 dozen | PREP 20 minutes | COOK 15 minutes

Ingredients

2 cups all-purpose flour

1 teaspoon salt

¼ teaspoon cayenne pepper

2 cups sharp Cheddar cheese, grated

14 tablespoons cold butter, cut into pieces

1 egg yolk

Pecan halves (approximately 2 dozen)

Directions

Whisk together the flour, salt, and cayenne pepper. Using a food processor, add the flour mixture, cheese, and butter and pulse to form a dough.

Roll out the dough on a floured surface to ¼-inch thickness. Use a small round cutter to form biscuits. Brush with beaten egg yolk and top with pecan halves.

Bake at 350 degrees for 10 to 15 minutes.

Notes

Lida was my neighbor and matriarch of our neighborhood. Many mornings after I dropped Elizabeth off at church school, I had to drop off Michael in his car seat at Lida's house, so I could get to work on time. Lida's cheese biscuits were always a welcome treat and will make a wonderful gift from your kitchen.

Hearty Vegetable Beef Soup

SERVES 10 | PREP 20 minutes | COOK 4 hours

Ingredients

1½ pounds bone-in short ribs

1½ pounds stew beef

Water

1 envelope of dry onion soup mix

1 (15-ounce) can tomato sauce

1 (16-ounce) can diced tomatoes

½ teaspoon garlic powder

½ teaspoon dried basil

½ teaspoon dried sage

½ teaspoon dried oregano

1 teaspoon black pepper

2 teaspoons salt

1 (15-ounce) package frozen soup mix vegetables

1 (10-ounce) can condensed tomato soup

Directions

Place ribs and stew beef in a 5-quart pot. Cover with water and simmer for 2½ hours.

Chill and then remove the fat and bones, carefully shredding the beef and returning it to the broth. Add dry onion soup mix, tomato sauce, tomatoes, garlic powder, basil, sage, oregano, pepper, and salt. Simmer for an hour.

Add vegetables and undiluted tomato soup. Simmer 30 minutes more.

Notes

This soup is even better the next day, so it's a great make-ahead. In fact, it must be made ahead. The soup has a lot of ingredients but takes very little actual prep time. It needs time to cook and simmer the wonderful flavors. It's delicious served with crusty bread or hot biscuits.

Creamy Broccoli Soup

SERVES 6 | PREP 20 minutes | COOK 30

Ingredients

¾ pound broccoli

¼ pound leeks

4 tablespoons (½ stick) butter

1 cup russet potatoes, peeled and diced

5 cups chicken broth

½ cup heavy cream

Salt and pepper

Directions

Separate the stalks from the broccoli tops. Chop both.

Wash the leeks and cut off the tops. Chop only the white part and discard the green part.

Sauté the chopped broccoli stalks and chopped leeks in the butter for about 3 minutes. Add broccoli tops and cook another 3 minutes.

Add potatoes and broth and bring to a boil. Cook 20 minutes.

Cool slightly. Puree in a blender and return to the soup pot. Stir in heavy cream. Season to taste with salt and pepper.

Notes

Baked Potato Soup

SERVES 8 | PREP 20 minutes | COOK 1 hour and 20 minutes

Ingredients

4 large baking potatoes

8 tablespoons (1 stick) butter

½ cup all-purpose flour

6 cups whole milk

1 teaspoon salt

½ teaspoon black pepper

½ cup green onions

¾ cup bacon, cooked and crumbled

½ cup Cheddar cheese, grated

1 (8-ounce) package sour cream

Directions

Bake potatoes at 400 degrees for 1 hour or until done. Cool. Dice and set aside.

Melt butter in heavy saucepan. Stir in the flour and cook 1 minute, stirring constantly. Gradually add milk, stirring constantly until thickened. Stir in salt and pepper.

Add diced potatoes and green onions. Serve with bacon, cheddar, and sour cream.

Notes

Crunchy Asian Spinach Salad

SERVES 10 | PREP 30 minutes

Ingredients

1 pound spinach, torn into bite-size pieces

½ pound white mushrooms, sliced

1 (8-ounce) can sliced water chestnuts, drained

1 cup bean sprouts, rinsed and drained

1 small white or yellow onion, thinly sliced and separated into rings

4 hard-cooked eggs

½ cup bacon, cooked and crumbled

Dressing:

½ cup extra virgin olive oil

⅓ cup sugar

3 tablespoons ketchup

3 tablespoons rice vinegar

2 tablespoons Worcestershire sauce

1 teaspoon soy sauce

½ teaspoon ground ginger

Directions

For the salad, combine the spinach, mushrooms, water chestnuts, bean sprouts, and onion. Just before serving, add the eggs, bacon, and dressing.

For the dressing, whisk together the oil, sugar, ketchup, vinegar, Worcestershire sauce, soy sauce, and ginger.

Notes

Ginger Orange Beef

SERVES 12 | PREP 30 minutes | COOK 10 minutes

Ingredients

3 pounds flank steak

2 tablespoons sesame oil

¼ cup fresh ginger, grated

3 carrots, diagonally sliced

2 red bell peppers, chopped

2 green bell peppers, chopped

2 cups sliced water chestnuts

8 ounces fresh snow peas, trimmed

2 tablespoons orange peel, grated

2 teaspoons cinnamon

⅓ cup soy sauce

1 tablespoon cornstarch

2 heads iceberg lettuce, shredded

Directions

Slice steak into strips. Heat oil in a large skillet or wok. Add steak and ginger. Stir-fry for 3 minutes or until steak is cooked through. Remove steak and keep warm. Add carrots and stir-fry for 1 minute. Add bell peppers, water chestnuts, snow peas, orange peel, and cinnamon. Stir-fry for 3 minutes or until vegetables are tender-crisp. Add steak.

In a small bowl, mix the soy sauce and cornstarch. Stir into the steak and vegetable mixture and cook until thickened, stirring constantly. Serve over the shredded lettuce.

Notes

John Boy and Billy's Chili

SERVES 6 | PREP 30 minutes | COOK 1 hour and 15 minutes

Ingredients

1 pound ground beef

1 green bell pepper, chopped

1 red bell pepper, chopped

1 yellow bell pepper, chopped

1 medium white or yellow onion, chopped

1 jalapeno pepper, chopped

½ teaspoon cayenne pepper

½ teaspoon red pepper flakes

1 teaspoon garlic powder

2 teaspoons ground cumin

1 (1.2-ounce) package chili seasoning mix

2 (16-ounce) cans red beans, undrained

1 (28-ounce) can diced tomatoes

1 (20-ounce) can tomato sauce

1 tablespoon honey

Corn chips

Grated sharp Cheddar cheese

Sour cream

Directions

In a large Dutch oven, brown the ground beef. Add the bell peppers, onions, jalapeno, cayenne pepper, and red pepper flakes. Stir in garlic powder, cumin, and chili seasoning. Add the beans, diced tomatoes, tomato sauce, and honey. Cover and simmer for 1 hour.

To serve, put corn chips in the bottom of a bowl and add chili. Top with cheddar cheese and sour cream to taste.

Notes

John Boy Isley and Bill James are among my favorite entertainers. They have been making morning radio more fun since the early '80s! They were always a joy to visit as we passed in the hallway at work. I loved having them make their great chili on TV with me.

Sesame Chicken Tacos

SERVES 4 to 6 | PREP 40 minutes | COOK 15 minutes

Ingredients

3 boned, skinless chicken breast halves

2 tablespoons soy sauce

Salt, to taste

½ cup cornstarch

2 tablespoons dark sesame oil

Sauce:

2 tablespoons honey

2 tablespoons soy sauce

1½ teaspoons cornstarch

1 tablespoon dark sesame oil

2 teaspoons rice vinegar

1 teaspoon chili paste

½ teaspoon garlic, minced

For serving:

8 (6-inch) flour tortillas, slightly warmed to soften

⅓ cup green onions

½ cup red bell pepper, sliced

¾ cup celery, sliced

½ cup dry roasted peanuts

Directions

Cut chicken breasts into bite-size pieces and place in a shallow dish. Add the soy sauce and coat each piece of chicken. Set aside for 30 minutes.

Remove chicken and discard marinade. Sprinkle with salt. Then roll each piece in cornstarch to coat.

Heat 2 tablespoons sesame oil in a large skillet. Cook chicken until done, turning as needed, about 10 minutes.

While the chicken is cooking, prepare the sauce by combining the honey, soy sauce, cornstarch, sesame oil, vinegar, chili paste, and garlic and heating in the microwave oven on high for 1 to 2 minutes or until thickened. Mix with chicken.

To serve, spoon a portion of the chicken into each warm tortilla and top with green onions, bell pepper, celery, and peanuts.

Notes

Dijon Sherry Chicken

SERVES 4 | PREP 20 minutes | COOK 30 minutes

Ingredients

4 boneless, skinless chicken breast halves

Salt and pepper, to taste

1 tablespoon butter

2 tablespoons extra virgin olive oil

½ cup shallots, chopped

⅓ cup dry sherry

2 teaspoons Dijon mustard

1 tablespoon fresh tarragon, chopped

¾ cup heavy cream

Freshly prepared rice

Directions

Sprinkle chicken breasts with salt and pepper.

Melt the butter with the oil in a large skillet. Brown the chicken on both sides, about 6 minutes. Remove the chicken to a plate while making the sauce.

Cook shallots in remaining oil and butter until soft. Stir in sherry and simmer for about 2 minutes. Whisk in broth, mustard, tarragon, and cream. Return chicken to the skillet and sauce. Reduce heat, cover, and simmer until the chicken is done and sauce has thickened, about 25 minutes.

Serve over rice.

Notes

Calabash Cove Crab Au Gratin

SERVES 2 | PREP 15 minutes | COOK 20 minutes

Ingredients

½ cup bread crumbs

3 tablespoons butter, melted and divided

2 tablespoons cream cheese, softened

1 tablespoon sour cream

1 tablespoon heavy cream

½ teaspoon all-purpose flour

½ teaspoon white wine

8 ounces fresh crabmeat

⅓ cup Cheddar cheese

Directions

Mix the bread crumbs with 1 tablespoon of melted butter. Set aside.

In a separate bowl, combine the cream cheese, sour cream, the remaining butter, heavy cream, flour, and wine. Mix until smooth.

Stir in the crabmeat. Spread into a small casserole dish or individual dishes.

Top with the buttered bread crumbs and Cheddar cheese.

Bake at 350 degrees until hot and bubbly, about 20 minutes. Increase baking time if made ahead and kept refrigerated.

Notes

Calabash Cove was a favorite restaurant for many years. They shared this delicious seafood recipe on my TV show. You can easily double it or triple it for the number of servings you need.

Sautéed Scallops with Pea Pods and Water Chestnuts

SERVES 4 to 6 | PREP 25 minutes | COOK 15 minutes

Ingredients

1½ pounds scallops

¼ cup dry sherry

3 tablespoons peanut oil

1 tablespoon fresh ginger, chopped

½ pound snow peas, trimmed

½ cup sliced water chestnuts

1 tablespoon oyster sauce

1 teaspoon dark sesame oil

1½ cups chicken stock

3 tablespoons cornstarch

¼ cup water

Salt and pepper, to taste

Directions

Rinse the scallops and pat dry. Pour the sherry over the scallops and let stand 10 minutes, then drain.

Heat peanut oil in skillet. Add scallops and ginger. Sauté 3 to 4 minutes.

Add snow peas, water chestnuts, oyster sauce, and sesame oil. Mix lightly. Pour in chicken stock and bring to a boil.

In a small bowl, whisk together the cornstarch and water to make a smooth paste. Stir into the scallop mixture.

Reduce heat and cook until sauce is thickened. Season to taste with salt and pepper.

Notes

Shrimp and Creamy Grits

SERVES 2 | PREP 30 minutes | COOK 20 minutes

Ingredients

Shrimp:

1 pound fresh shrimp, peeled and deveined

2 tablespoons lemon juice

Hot pepper sauce, to taste

Salt and black pepper, to taste

3 tablespoons bacon drippings

½ cup Vidalia onion, chopped

½ cup green bell pepper, chopped

2 tablespoons flour

¾ cup chicken broth

Grits:

2 cups milk

¼ teaspoon salt

2 tablespoons butter

½ cup uncooked grits

½ to 1 cup half-and-half

Directions

Combine the shrimp, lemon juice, hot pepper sauce, salt, and black pepper. Set aside.

In a large skillet, heat the bacon drippings. Cook the onion and bell pepper until soft, stirring constantly. Sprinkle the flour over the onions and peppers and cook, stirring constantly until the flour browns lightly. Add shrimp and broth, stirring until the shrimp turn pink and the sauce is thick and smooth. If the sauce becomes too thick, add more broth.

For the grits, combine the milk, salt, butter, and grits in a heavy saucepan. Bring to a low boil, reduce heat and simmer until thickened, stirring occasionally. Stir in half-and-half until creamy.

Serve shrimp over the grits.

Notes

I received the most beautiful message on Facebook from a young woman whose mom had been a regular viewer of my show. Sharon Dunn shared that her mom had given her my recipe for Shrimp and Grits. She said it was the best she had ever eaten and that included the fine restaurants in New York where Sharon became a Ford Model, the most prestigious modeling agency in the world. This one's for you, Sharon.

La Strada Pasta Salad

SERVES 4 to 6 | PREP 25 minutes | COOK 10 minutes

Ingredients

4 cups cooked penne pasta, cooled

⅓ cup balsamic vinaigrette dressing (your favorite brand or homemade will work well)

2 tablespoons pesto sauce (your favorite prepared or homemade pesto will work well)

4 ounces feta cheese, crumbled

¼ cup frozen green peas, thawed in cool water and drained

3 tablespoons carrots, finely grated

2 tablespoons green onions, diced

3 tablespoons green bell pepper, chopped

2 tablespoons walnuts, chopped

2 tablespoons sweetened dried cranberries, chopped

Directions

Add balsamic dressing to pasta and gently mix.

Add pesto and gently mix.

Add crumbled feta cheese and toss.

Then add peas, carrots, onions, bell peppers, walnuts, and cranberries and toss

If preparing in advance, the pasta will soak into the dressing, so you may wish to add a bit more dressing just before serving if the mix becomes too dry. Add small amounts of dressing at a time and toss. Too much dressing will mask the wonderful complex tastes.

Notes

I enjoyed countless delicious meals at La Strada Italian Grill in Charlotte. You can now enjoy fantastic brick-oven pizzas, pasta, salads, and more at Dixie and Joe Mazur's Lake Lure, North Carolina, location where Patrick Swayze made us fall in love with *Dirty Dancing.*

Seafood Fettuccine

SERVES 4 | PREP 20 minutes | COOK 15 minutes

Ingredients

2 tablespoons butter

2 cups uncooked seafood (shrimp, scallops, fish, or a combination)

½ teaspoon salt

½ teaspoon black pepper

½ teaspoon nutmeg

2 teaspoons all-purpose flour

12 ounces cooked fettuccine, kept hot

¾ cup heavy cream

½ cup Parmesan cheese

Directions

Heat butter in a large skillet. Add the seafood, salt, pepper, nutmeg, and flour. Cook and stir for 1 minute or until the seafood is done. Add the hot fettuccine and heavy cream, stirring constantly until thickened and the pasta is well coated. Sprinkle with cheese.

Notes

Sheri Lynch's Pasta with Fresh Tomatoes

SERVES 4 | PREP 20 minutes | COOK 15 minutes

Ingredients

2 pounds ripe tomatoes, peeled and cut into bite-size chunks

⅓ cup extra virgin olive oil

12 leaves fresh basil, minced

2 cloves garlic, minced

¼ cup fresh parsley, finely chopped

¼ cup black olives, sliced

Coarse black pepper and salt, to taste

1 (1-pound) box angel-hair pasta

Freshly ground Romano cheese, to taste

Directions

Combine the tomatoes, oil, basil, garlic, parsley, and olives. Add salt and pepper to taste. Set aside for at least 2 hours or refrigerate overnight (the longer, the better).

Before serving, let the sauce come to room temperature.

Cook the pasta al dente according to package directions, rinse with hot water, and drain.

Toss with tomatoes. Sprinkle with cheese.

Excellent as a light main course or as a side dish with fish or chicken.

Notes

Sheri Lynch is one of the most popular and delightful radio personalities in the country. Before she was "discovered," she kept me entertained while producing commercials for me. She is one of the most talented humans I have ever known. She's also brilliant, loves animals, and can cook.

Baked Vidalia Onions

SERVES 8 | PREP 20 minutes | COOK 20 minutes

Ingredients

6 large Vidalia onions, sliced

⅓ cup butter, melted

Salt and pepper, to taste

½ teaspoon sugar

½ cup vermouth

1 teaspoon Worcestershire sauce

½ cup Gruyère cheese, grated

½ cup bread crumbs

1 teaspoon paprika

2 tablespoons butter, melted

Directions

In a large skillet, cook the onions in the ⅓ cup butter until soft. Sprinkle with salt, pepper, and sugar. Add vermouth and Worcestershire sauce. Cook for about 3 minutes, stirring frequently.

Spread into a 9 x 13-inch baking dish. Sprinkle with cheese.

Combine bread crumbs, paprika, and remaining butter. Bake at 350 degrees for 20 minutes.

Notes

Elvis Presley Pound Cake

SERVES 15 | PREP 20 minutes | COOK 1 hour

Ingredients

1 cup (2 sticks) butter, softened

3 cups sugar

7 eggs

3 cups cake flour

1 cup heavy cream

2 teaspoons vanilla extract

¼ teaspoon almond extract

Directions

Bring ingredients to room temperature. Beat the butter and sugar until light and fluffy. Add eggs one at a time beating well after each. Alternate adding small portions of the flour and the heavy cream to the egg mixture. Add vanilla and almond extracts.

Grease and flour one very large Bundt or tube pan (or two slightly smaller tube pans). Pour the batter into the prepared pan(s) and bake at 325 degrees for about 1 hour and 10 minutes or until it springs to the touch. Cool in pan about 5 minutes before turning out onto a platter.

Notes

Roasted Vegetables Parmesan

SERVES 6 | PREP 20 minutes | COOK 15 to 20 minutes

Ingredients

1½ cups white or yellow onions, sliced

1½ teaspoons garlic, minced

2 cups carrots, sliced

2 cups broccoli florets

2 cups cauliflower florets

½ cup celery, sliced

Extra virgin olive oil

2 tablespoons parsley, minced

3 tablespoons white wine

2 tablespoons Parmesan cheese, grated

Directions

Combine the onions, garlic, carrots, broccoli, cauliflower, and celery in a large bowl. Toss with just enough olive oil to coat all the vegetables. (Brussels sprouts are also delicious prepared this way.)

Line a shallow baking pan with foil. Spread the vegetables over the foil. Sprinkle with the parsley and white wine.

Roast at 425 degrees until the edges begin to brown and the vegetables are tender, about 15 minutes. Stir a couple of times during the roasting.

Sprinkle with cheese.

Notes

Cheerwine Cake

SERVES 16 | PREP 20 minutes | COOK 30 minutes

Ingredients

1 box devil's food cake mix

1 cup Cheerwine (cherry-flavored soda)

1 teaspoon almond extract

Frosting:

⅓ cup Cheerwine (cherry-flavored soda)

8 tablespoons (1 stick) butter

¼ cup unsweetened cocoa powder

¼ teaspoon almond extract

2½ cups powdered sugar

1 cup pecans, chopped (optional)

Directions

Prepare the cake mix according to package directions substituting 1 cup of Cheerwine for the water and adding almond extract. Grease and flour a 9 x 13-inch cake pan. Pour the batter into the prepared pan. Bake as directed on package.

For the frosting, place the powdered sugar in a mixing bowl. Heat the Cheerwine, butter, and cocoa in a saucepan, mixing well. Bring to a boil, then lower heat and simmer for 1 minute. Remove from heat and stir in the ¼ teaspoon almond extract. Pour mixture over the powdered sugar and blend until smooth. Add pecans (optional). Spread over cake.

Notes

Cheerwine is an iconic Southern soft drink created in North Carolina over 100 years ago. The name comes from its fizzy wild-cherry taste and burgundy color. It is a Southern treasure. Restaurant critic Alan Richman wrote in a 2006 article for GQ.com, "Cheerwine is pretty much the sweetest soft drink ever made, and in my opinion the greatest accompaniment to barbecue ever produced." If you must, Dr. Pepper or a generic cherry-flavored soda would work in this recipe.

Killer Key Lime Pie

SERVES 6 | PREP 30 minutes | COOK 30 minutes

Ingredients

Crust:

1¼ cups graham cracker crumbs

¼ cup sugar

¼ teaspoon cinnamon

6 tablespoons butter, melted

Filling:

5 egg yolks, beaten

1 (14-ounce) can sweetened condensed milk

½ cup key lime juice

Whipped cream

Fresh limes

Directions

For the crust, combine the graham cracker crumbs, sugar, cinnamon, and butter and mix well. Press into a 9-inch pie plate. Bake at 375 degrees for 8 minutes. Cool slightly while making the filling.

For the filling, combine the egg yolks, sweetened condensed milk, and lime juice. Pour into the prepared graham cracker crust. Bake at 375 degrees for 15 minutes.

Cool completely. Top each slice with whipped cream, a lime slice, and freshly grated lime peel.

Notes

In Ian Fleming's books, James Bond was a fan of key lime pie. My husband Mike and I attended the world premiere of the movie *Licence to Kill* starring Timothy Dalton. Prince Charles and Princess Diana attended. Seeing them in the theater was far more exciting to me than the movie. Afterward, there was a beautiful dinner event where I met the stars and enjoyed delicious "James Bond food" including key lime pie.

My friend Casey Ballard from Lancaster, South Carolina, shared his version of this wonderful dessert with me.

"This upheaval never for a second shook my Christian faith. It strengthened it. I praised God for the privilege of doing something I loved for decades, let Him know I was excited about whatever was coming next, and prayed that He would provide. He did."

Barbara McKay

Spoonfuls of Goodness

I view life as one big bowl of yummy flavors just waiting to be tasted. Every now and then, something a little too bitter or too sour comes along. But a nice palette cleanser has me ready to dive back in!

Reflections

Moving On..................142
Life without Daily TV........143
Clients Were Always Friends 148
Animal Advocacy............151
My Passion for Fashion.....154

Moving On

Mike went on to a job he adores. Radio was always his first love. His first broadcasting job began at a station in Tennessee at age fourteen. While most men his age now are retired, he is still doing the job he loves every single day. He is the morning host at WDAV 89.9 on the campus of Davidson College. It's his favorite job ever, and he treasures each day with his coworkers and the listeners who love classical music and him. WDAV is recognized as one of the best classical stations in the country and is also one of the highest rated, thanks to the Internet. Mike regularly hears from listeners locally, nationally, and globally. It is always a special treat when he hears from composers who appreciate his work.

My entrepreneurial spirit, inherited from my father, along with my need for flexible hours has brought many wonderful experiences and new friends. Had I continued my demanding daily television routine, I would have missed out on some exciting, rewarding, and fun adventures. Though I must acknowledge that without that daily routine for decades, many of these opportunities would not have happened. Everything happens for a reason and in its own season. Never forget that.

Not all of my adventures turned out as successfully as I had hoped, but they all taught me meaningful and important lessons and brought special people into my life.

Everything happens for a reason and in its own season. Never forget that.

Life without Daily TV

It was time to get down to work. Just because it wasn't daily TV doesn't mean it wasn't on camera. Because of my grocery store ties and their marketing agencies for their products, I was hired for national media tours. Appearing on stations and meeting new TV viewers all over the country was another adventure for me. I enjoyed telling people about new grocery stores, Target stores, Lowe's home improvement stores, Tyson Chicken, and many others. I especially loved working for Lowe's because when I was growing up, my father built the very first Lowe's stores. Things happen for a reason. Tyson Chicken was another favorite because I really enjoyed visiting their headquarters in Arkansas. This huge empire is located in a rural area where chickens seem to roam freely. The people were so down-to-earth and welcoming; it made me feel like I was back at my grandparent's farm but with a big board room.

This is probably the most well-known photo of me thanks to my extraordinarily talented clients and friends Ross and Debra Nash. Dr. Ross Nash is one of the most celebrated cosmetic dentists in the world and teaches other dentists through the

Nash Institute. Dr. Nash transformed my teeth before I even knew they needed it. Debra, his wife, is a marketing genius.

We were taking photos with the very talented, nationally known photographer Deborah Triplett for an ad campaign. We were all wrapped up, and I was about to leave. As I was putting on my sunglasses and saying goodbye, Debra Nash shouted, "Stop! Wait. Deborah, snap that." She did. Hundreds of thousands have seen that photo, and it is one of my all-time favorites. And so are the Nashes. We have stayed forever friends. You will read in a later chapter about my life-changing accident. The Nashes were instrumental in my recovery and not just my teeth.

Diamonds Direct was another great client. What a joy it has been to represent beautiful diamond jewelry for some the kindest people of integrity I have ever met—Itay, Dovey, Crystal, Kelly, and Boaz. It thrills me to help a business that truly deserves it to grow and to help friends get the best prices on forever treasures. Win-win-win.

I continued cooking on TV for local shows across the country and then took my food, fashion, and other passions to magazines. I wrote restaurant reviews for *SouthPark* magazine for eight years. It was

I was blessed to start my next venture with happy memories and wonderful new friendships, experiences, and knowledge.

delicious and fun getting to enjoy Charlotte restaurants and the fine people who created them. After writing for other magazines, Fred Jacob from Knoxville, Tennessee, approached me about doing my own magazines. He is a successful publisher who taught me the magazine industry. We had lots of fun doing *Barbara McKay's Simply the*

Best as well as my bridal magazine. I was privileged to meet many talented people and learn the intricacies of industries through my advertisers. When the Great Recession hit in 2008, my publishing career ended, but I was blessed to start my next venture with happy memories and wonderful new friendships, experiences, and knowledge.

"My wish for you is that you continue. Continue to be who you are, to astonish a mean world with your acts of kindness."

– Maya Angelou

Though my magazine publishing days were over, my interest in sharing good information that people could use was not. Debbie Williams is a talented marketing genius and shares

Spending time with Ms. Angelou as she shared her wisdom was priceless.

Photo By: Katherina Aquino Xtreme Talents School of Arts 2017

my work ethic. She and I produced TV shows on a variety of topics helpful to consumers. *Simply the Best* aired on several stations.

One of the most memorable events in my life happened in 2008 when the magnificent Maya Angelou named me as a recipient of her Women Who Lead awards. When I received the letter telling me I had been chosen, I feared it was a mistake. I called her office to make sure it was for real. Spending time with Ms. Angelou as she shared her wisdom was priceless. The award was presented at a huge banquet in her honor with hundreds of women wearing fabulous hats. I will never forget that special day.

Clients Were Always Friends

During this time of working closely with many wonderful companies, something very special and intriguing happened.

I was honored to do commercials and special events for Boyles Furniture for many years. One of their top employees is one of my most-favorite people in the world. Curtis Fortner is loved by every person who knows him. He inspires, encourages, makes you think, and best of all, makes you laugh. He is the best kind of friend who will always be there no matter what.

When my mother died, her funeral was quite a way from Curtis's home. He not only showed up to support and comfort me but also made me laugh hysterically—not easy at your mother's funeral. He showed up carrying a famous wildlife artist's rendering of an opossum. Who and why would someone do that? Thoughtful Curtis would. He knew that every night I fed a sweet opossum in my backyard that I had come to love and named Matthew. I always gave Matthew cover in my attic when it rained or was terribly cold. He would climb a tree, leap to my roof, and then climb up to another part of the roof where he found an opening to enter. Most people don't find opossums loveable, but Curtis knew I did. That signed and numbered opossum portrait has proudly been on display at my home since he carried it into my mom's funeral. Curtis has also agreed to speak at my funeral, or I at his, depending on who goes first.

Curtis also introduced me to another favorite, fascinating, and special person in my life which led me to a very interesting discovery.

Scene & Heard

AROUND TOWN
WITH OLIVIA FORTSON

BETH COSNER PHOTOGRAPHY

Earl Charles Spencer

Earl Charles Spencer, brother of the late Princess Diana (from left); Barbara McKay; and Curtis Fortner, manager of Boyles Furniture at Carolina Place, attend a special event on May 28 at Boyles. Earl Spencer spoke about Althorp, one of the great country houses of Britain and home to the Spencer family for more than 500 years. He joined Theodore Alexander to make the designs from the Spencer furniture collection at Althorp available to the public. The resulting Althorp collection is showcased at Boyles.

Boyles Furniture was selling reproductions of the beautiful antiques from Princess Diana's magnificent childhood home, Althorp. A writer for the *Los Angeles Times* once wrote that Althorp "makes Downton Abbey look like Downton *Shabby*." British nobleman Charles the 9th Earl of Spencer, Princess Diana's brother who currently owns and resides at Althorp, was coming to the United States to speak and represent his family's Althorp Collection of finely crafted reproductions. Curtis said they needed someone to facilitate Charles's appearances, which meant introducing him and hosting these special events with him. Of course, I was honored to be asked and looked forward to meeting Charles, especially after watching his moving tribute to his sister at her funeral.

After all he had been through, I was expecting a somber, stoic, formal, unflappable British nobleman. But within five minutes of being introduced, I realized that Earl Charles Spencer is truly warm, kind, smart, down-to earth, and very talented. What a joy it was for me to work with this good-natured, witty, and fun man. He captivated his audience. People loved seeing, buying, and collecting these heirloom pieces from his family's historic home. Charles uses the inspiring Althorp Collection to continue his sister's charitable legacy.

In between our appearances, he and I enjoyed sharing serious life stories, as well as laughing a lot. It was interesting how quickly and easily our personalities clicked. We became trusted, friends. My daughter Elizabeth and I visited Charles at Althorp in

London, and he still comes to North Carolina where we can visit in High Point. Email makes communicating easy. Many things have changed in our lives, but our surprisingly special friendship remains. Something very interesting happened later that might explain our becoming trusted friends so quickly, even though we are from totally different worlds.

A couple of years ago my son, Michael, gave me Ancestry.com for Mother's Day. After researching for a few months, suddenly there it was—a *Spencer* in my family tree. I checked and rechecked the lineage three times looking at birth and marriage certificates and all the other documented proof provided by Ancestry. I didn't want to contact Charles until I had all the correct information. Then I emailed Charles and shared my findings. Within moments, I heard back from him with the greeting, "Well hello, Cousin."

Yes, there is order in this world. And God winked again.

Yes, there is order in this world. And God winked again.

Animal Advocacy

I inherited my grandmother's passion and love for animals. She lived on a farm and at all times had a menagerie of domestic and wild animals. She took in all the abandoned cats and dogs that seemed to find their way to her remote farmhouse and barn. Along with her pets and farm animals, wild animals would congregate and liked to stick around. Mama White was like Snow White with birds fluttering around her and little furry creatures hovering at her feet. One of the most intriguing was a little skunk who adored her and followed her around for eight years like a cat. My grandmother would be pleased to know that God gave me that same heart for animals. *I adore them.*

Before Mike and I downsized to a smaller home, wild animals gathered in my yard every night even though I lived right in the middle of the busy SouthPark area of Charlotte. Each night in my backyard, I fed raccoons, opossums, and deer. They came with their families all at the same time. They had no problem getting along, which amazed me. I set up pine straw, a little cedar house, and blankets in my storage house. I heated special microwaveable pads to nestle under the straw and blankets during winter. The hardest part of moving from that house after twenty-seven years was leaving my animals behind.

One of my most interesting animal stories is hard to believe. I was so happy that I had witnesses. I am very wary of hawks because they are predators of little furry animals. But there was a hawk who seemed determined to win me over. Each day he followed me along my two-mile walk. I have to admit that he was a beautiful bird, but I was a little distant. When I got back home, he would perch just outside my kitchen window. He probably snickered the first time I saw him there and jumped and yelped. He nearly hurt himself one day when I was sitting on my patio. He came swooping down toward me, could not stop in time, and crashed into my window. He fell to the ground but shook it off and then took off. I think he was embarrassed. He stayed away for a few days. But soon he was back and did his most daring act yet to attract my attention. I was walking, and he was following along a busy street. Suddenly, he swooped down, scooped up a squirrel, flew directly to me, and dropped the squirrel on me. A stranger was walking his dog behind me and was stunned. He kept shouting how shocking it was to see what that hawk did. I told him I knew that hawk, and he did things like that to show off and impress me.

I share these few of my many animal stories because it's this love for animals that led me to another important part of my life: animal rescue. Not doing

TV every day gave me the chance to help needy animals. As I've said many times, our precious pets, both dogs and cats, seem to have the qualities God hoped for us: unconditional love and forgiveness. Through my work as an animal advocate, I have gotten to know some of the most incredibly wonderful people in rescue. I urge all of you to find out about this rewarding way to make a difference in this world.

I'm on the board of one of the most amazing animal rescues. These fantastic, giving, caring people from the rescue *Clifford's Army* are led by Deb Hardin in Shelby, North Carolina. It is named after the first dog they saved. Find them on Facebook. They do daring, bold, dangerous things to save dogs, and I am in awe of them. They told me what they would like to name their TV show if I can ever make it happen: *Redneck Rescue*. I *love* these smart, brave, generous heroes and love spending time with them. I could (and should) write a book about their miraculous adventures.

I also volunteer with the Humane Society of Charlotte raising money to build a new facility. My son generously made a donation, which earned him the right to name a portion of the new building. Michael chose to name the men's bathroom in honor of Peeve, his cat growing up.

My Passion for Fashion

I've had a passion for fashion every day since I can remember. My beautiful mom was often told she looked like the star Natalie Wood. To me, she dressed like a movie star and was often featured in our local newspaper modeling beautiful outfits. I always wanted to look like her, but that never happened. So I just tried to dress like her.

From the time I was a toddler, she dressed me like a little lady, not in ruffles, sequins, and bows, but in hats, gloves, and tailored coats. She created clothes from images I found in magazines. I enjoyed those handmade treasures through high school. After college, I asked her to invest in a clothing store for me to own. She laughed and said, "No way. You don't want to *run* a store. You want to be

That desire to dress up has never left me.

able to meet designers and have a store *as your closet*." Her part in my TV career allowed me to meet those designers many years later.

That desire to dress up has never left me. Those of you who see me out and about, whether grocery shopping or going for walks, know I am always a little dressed up. I like it. It reminds me of my mom. She was always telling me, "When you look good, you do good," which is just an abbreviated way of saying that looking your best, leads you to feeling your best, which leads to doing your best. It's empowering—feeling confident and strong and being able to do your best whether it's your job or helping others. A favorite little quote of mine is, "When I like my outfit, I'm nicer." I think that is probably more true than some would like to admit.

Photo and Styling By: Keith Hamilton and Mandii Green

A very special friend, whom I admire so much, has had a paramount part in keeping me empowered. She genuinely understands that it's not just about clothes. After all these decades in the media, she has helped me reinvent myself to remain relevant while remaining authentic to who I am. Not an easy task. I am just one of many whose lives have been touched and changed for the better by the extraordinary Laura Vinroot Poole.

Over two decades ago, Laura had a vision for a designer clothing store. Capitol was created. I was Laura's very first customer. While it is now known around the world for the most beautifully curated collection of designer clothing, accessories, jewelry, and shoes, Laura's vision was not to create a store for those obsessed with clothes, but a business to help people feel good about themselves. She genuinely helps us evolve, stay young, and wear what makes us our best selves.

Because of Laura's genuine altruistic approach to business, Capitol has become a crown jewel in the fashion kingdom. With all of her success, Laura has never forgotten that I was her first customer and continues to allow me to enjoy her success and spend time with some of my most-favorite famous people—fashion designers.

Their personal stories, hard work, and motivations are as beautiful and colorful as their clothes. I've been able to meet and get to know them at Capitol. Besides admiring beautiful, colorful, classic-with-a-twist clothes made of fine fabrics, I buy and wear clothes not because of a label but because of the kind of person and the talent behind that label. How

Their personal stories, hard work, and motivations are as beautiful and colorful as their clothes.

Photo and Styling By: Keith Hamilton and Mandii Green

that garment came to be makes it far more appealing to me. I love to wear designers whose character, kindness, and love for people inspire their designs and their work.

I am so fortunate to have met one of those extraordinary designers decades earlier. Oscar de la Renta was such a prince of a man. His designs were elegant, beautiful treasures, and so was the man. This lovely gentleman seemed like royalty. Along with being one of the most well-known and talented designers in history, he was also known

for his kindness and generosity for philanthropic causes.

I was thrilled when he came to my TV show and I got to interview him. He was in town for *Serenade to Autumn*, the fashion show produced annually by Belk. It was as fabulous as any New York or Paris show. My husband Mike and I hosted it for years. I enjoyed meeting many designers through that experience, but no one was more impressive than this man. I taped an interview with Mr. de la Renta at 9:00 a.m. in the studio because live models were involved. For the sake of time (models have to change), we needed to tape and edit it.

Being a fashion fanatic, I could hardly believe I was sitting and talking with *the* Oscar de la Renta. He was as lovely as you would expect. I was star struck and mesmerized by every word. After we finished around 10:30, I thanked him profusely and said goodbye, expecting him to be whisked away in his limo. He smiled and said, "I can stay and watch your live show." He was so very down-to-earth and seemed genuinely interested to stay and watch. WOW! I loved getting to know him and hearing his wonderful stories off camera.

After our live show ended at noon, I thanked him again and felt more like he was a friend and not just a superstar. I explained I had to race off to my radio show at 1:00. To my surprise, Oscar said that he could listen and be a part of that show too. This man just kept wowing me. I expressed my excitement and apologized that I would have to run down to the cafeteria and grab a sandwich because I needed energy to keep talking on the radio. And then this prince shocked me again. He said that sounded good. So Oscar de la Renta, one of the most famous designers in the world, shared a pimiento cheese sandwich with me and then appeared on the radio with

me. That tells you the kind of man he was.

A few new favorites and legends in the making are Mira Mikati, Barbara Tfank, Irene Neuwirth, Lela Rose, Marion Parke, Jane Pendry (Dovima Paris). Look them up and read about them. They all have such fascinating stories. My passion for fashion is about so much more than just clothes.

So Oscar de la Renta, one of the most famous designers in the world, shared a pimiento cheese sandwich with me and then appeared on the radio with me. That tells you the kind of man he was.

New Favorite Recipes

Even though I don't share recipes on TV every day, I still enjoy discovering new ones to share with my family and friends, as well as on my blog at BarbaraMcKay.com.

Spicy Toasted Pecans....................162
Great Guacamole..........................163
Spicy Black Bean Soup..................164
Favorite Onion Soup......................165
Hot Spiced Cider..........................167
Tomato Bisque.............................168
Cornucopia Salad.........................169
Curried Rice Salad........................170
Lemon Ginger Chicken Salad...........171
Black Bean Salsa..........................172
Almond and Vegetable Stir Fry..........173
Caramelized Onions......................174
Cranberry Barbecued Chicken..........175
Barbecued Chicken and Avocado Salad..........177
Chicken Quesadilla.......................178
Macadamia Mahi Mahi...................179
Baked Salmon.............................181
4-Ingredient Cheese Biscuits...........183
Cheesy Garlic Bread.....................184
Gourmet Grilled Cheese Sandwich.....185
Zebra Crème Brûlée.....................186
Hot Fudge Sauce.........................187
Caramel Sauce...........................188
Chocolate Gravy.........................189

Spicy Toasted Pecans

MAKES 5 cups | PREP 15 minutes | COOK 20 minutes

Ingredients

5 cups pecan halves

4 tablespoons butter

1 tablespoon ground cumin

½ teaspoon cayenne pepper

¼ cup sugar

1½ teaspoons salt

Directions

Place the pecans in a mixing bowl.

In a small saucepan, melt the butter and stir in the cumin and cayenne pepper until mixed well. Pour over the pecans and toss well. Sprinkle sugar and salt over the pecans. Stir to coat.

Spread the pecans in a foil-lined baking pan. Bake at 300 degrees until toasted, stirring occasionally, for about 20 minutes. Cool. Store in an airtight container.

Notes

Great Guacamole

SERVES 6 to 8 | PREP 15 minutes

Ingredients

4 ripe avocados

Juice of 1 lime

1 teaspoon coarse sea salt

½ cup red onion, diced

4 tablespoons fresh cilantro, chopped

⅔ cup ripe tomato, chopped

½ teaspoon garlic, minced

Dash cayenne pepper

Tortilla chips

Directions

Peel, pit, and mash the avocados. Place in a medium mixing bowl. Stir in the lime juice, salt, onion, cilantro, tomato, garlic, and cayenne pepper.

Serve with chips.

Notes

I also enjoy this as a sandwich spread on toasted dark pumpernickel or multigrain bread.

Spicy Black Bean Soup

SERVES 4 to 6 | PREP 20 minutes | COOK 5 minutes

Ingredients

1 tablespoon extra virgin olive oil

½ cup white or yellow onion, chopped

½ cup celery, chopped

1 clove garlic, minced

1 tablespoon chili powder

2 teaspoons ground cumin

1½ cups vegetable broth

2 (15.5-ounce) cans black beans

½ cup fresh salsa

Salt and pepper, to taste

Sour cream and chopped avocado for garnish

Directions

Heat the oil in a soup pot. Sauté the onion, celery, and garlic until tender. Stir in chili powder and cumin. Add the broth and one can of the beans. Heat thoroughly.

Puree the remaining can of beans and then add to the soup pot. Cook for 5 minutes. Stir in salsa and simmer until thickened. Add salt and pepper to taste.

Serve with sour cream and chopped avocado.

Notes

Favorite Onion Soup

SERVES 6 | PREP 25 minutes | COOK 45 minutes

Ingredients

8 tablespoons (1 stick) butter

4 medium white or yellow onions, thinly sliced

6 shallots, minced

2 teaspoons sugar

3 tablespoons all-purpose flour

6 cups beef stock

⅓ cup dry sherry

Salt and pepper, to taste

1 cup heavy cream

⅓ cup Parmesan cheese, shredded

⅓ cup mozzarella cheese, shredded

Directions

Melt butter in a large saucepan and add onions. Cook slowly until golden, about 5 minutes. Stir in shallots and sugar. Cook 2 more minutes.

Sprinkle in flour and cook, stirring constantly for 1 minute. Slowly stir in 2 cups of the beef broth and heat for 5 minutes, stirring frequently.

Remove from heat. Puree in a blender or food processor. Return to pan and add remaining stock. Bring to a boil, then reduce heat and simmer 15 minutes more. Add sherry and cook 5 minutes.

Season with salt and pepper. Pour soup into ovenproof bowls.

Whip cream. Fold the cheeses into the whipped cream.

Top soup with cream mixture. Broil on low until lightly browned.

Notes

Hot Spiced Cider

MAKES 1 gallon | PREP 15 minutes | COOK 15 minutes

Ingredients

1 gallon apple cider (filtered if available)

2 cups pineapple juice

2 cups orange juice

½ cup lemon juice

1 cup sugar

4 teaspoons pumpkin pie spice

Cinnamon sticks and/or Orange slices for garnish

Directions

Combine the cider, juices, sugar, pumpkin pie spice, and cinnamon sticks in a Dutch oven. Bring to a boil. Whisk to dissolve sugar and blend spices. Reduce heat and simmer for 10 minutes.

Serve hot with cinnamon sticks and/or orange slices. Store in refrigerator. When serving, reheat on a stove top or in the microwave.

Notes

Tomato Bisque

SERVES 6 | PREP 20 minutes | COOK 20 minutes

Ingredients

3 cups tomato juice

1 (28-ounce) can whole tomatoes, drained

2 cups chicken stock

⅓ cup basil leaves, loosely packed

10 tablespoons butter, cut into pieces

1½ cups heavy cream

½ teaspoon salt

½ teaspoon black pepper

Parmesan cheese, grated

Directions

In a large saucepan, combine the tomato juice, canned tomatoes, and chicken stock. Simmer for 10 minutes.

Mix in basil leaves. Puree mixture a little at a time in a food processor or blender and return to saucepan.

On low heat, whisk in the butter and stir until melted. Stir in cream and whisk until heated through. Season with salt and pepper.

Serve with grated Parmesan cheese.

Notes

Cornucopia Salad

SERVES 4 | PREP 20 minutes

Ingredients

1 large head of leafy lettuce, chopped

4 green onions, sliced

1 (11-ounce) can mandarin oranges, drained

1 Honeycrisp apple, coarsely diced

⅓ cup sweetened dried cranberries

½ cup goat cheese, crumbled

1 ripe avocado, peeled, pitted, and sliced

½ cup sugared pecans or almonds (the ““Sweet and Spicy Roasted Pecans” on page 27 are great in this recipe)

Dressing:

¼ cup extra virgin olive oil

2 tablespoons apple cider vinegar

2 tablespoons sugar

½ teaspoon salt

½ teaspoon black pepper

1 tablespoon fresh parsley, chopped

Directions

In a large bowl, toss together the lettuce, onions, oranges, apple, cranberries, cheese, avocado and nuts. At serving time, add the dressing, which can be made ahead of time.

For the dressing, whisk together the oil, vinegar, sugar, salt, pepper, and parsley.

Notes

Curried Rice Salad

SERVES 6 | PREP 20 minutes | COOK 20 minutes

Ingredients

1 cup uncooked rice

½ cup dried cherries, chopped

¼ cup mayonnaise

¼ cup mango chutney

1 teaspoon curry powder

⅓ cup slivered almonds, toasted

1 pear, chopped

½ cup seedless grapes, halved

2 teaspoons fresh lemon juice

Directions

Cook rice according to package directions, drain, and cool.

Stir in cherries, mayonnaise, chutney, and curry powder. Cover and chill.

Just before serving, stir in the almonds, pear, grapes, and lemon juice. Serve chilled.

Notes

Lemon Ginger Chicken Salad

SERVES 6 | PREP 25 minutes | COOK

Ingredients

Dressing:

½ cup mayonnaise

¼ cup sour cream

1 teaspoon sugar

1 teaspoon lemon peel, freshly grated

1 tablespoon lemon juice

½ teaspoon ground ginger

¼ teaspoon salt

Salad:

2 cups chicken, cooked and chopped

1 cup celery, sliced

Romaine lettuce or mixed greens, torn into bite-size pieces

½ cup seedless grapes, halved

½ cup roasted pecans (the "Sweet and Spicy Roasted Pecans" on page 27 are great in this recipe)

½ cup sweetened dried cranberries

Directions

Prepare the dressing in a small mixing bowl by combining the mayonnaise, sour cream, sugar, lemon peel, lemon juice, ginger, and salt. Mix well. Set aside.

In a medium mixing bowl, toss together the chicken and celery. Stir in the dressing. Chill.

Serve over salad greens. Top the salad with grapes, pecans, and cranberries.

Notes

Black Bean Salsa

SERVES 12 | PREP 15 minutes

Ingredients

Salsa:

1 (15-ounce) can corn

1 (15-ounce) can black beans

2 cloves garlic, minced

⅓ cup white or yellow onion, chopped

⅓ cup red bell pepper, chopped

⅓ cup green bell pepper, chopped

½ avocado, peeled, pitted, and chopped

⅓ cup cilantro, chopped

Dressing:

2 tablespoons fresh lime juice

1 tablespoon honey

1 teaspoon ground cumin

1 teaspoon hot pepper sauce

1 teaspoon rice vinegar

Salt to taste

Directions

In a large mixing bowl, combine corn, black beans, garlic, onion, bell peppers, avocado, and cilantro.

In a separate bowl, whisk together the lime juice, honey, cumin, pepper sauce, vinegar, and salt. Pour over the bean mixture.

Notes

Almond and Vegetable Stir Fry

SERVES 4 | PREP 20 minutes | COOK 10 minutes

Ingredients

1 cup carrots, sliced

1 cup fresh green beans, cut in 1-inch pieces

1 tablespoon extra virgin olive oil

1 cup cauliflower crowns, sliced

½ cup green onions, sliced

1 cup chicken broth

2 teaspoons cornstarch

⅛ teaspoon garlic powder

¼ cup sliced almonds

Directions

Sauté the carrots and green beans in oil for 2 minutes. Add the cauliflower and green onions and cook for 3 minutes, stirring constantly.

In a medium bowl, combine the chicken broth, cornstarch, and garlic powder. Add to vegetables and cook, stirring frequently for about 3 more minutes or until thickened. Stir in almonds.

Notes

Caramelized Onions

MAKES about 1½ cups | PREP 10 minutes | COOK 35 minutes

Ingredients

2 large white or yellow onions, sliced

2 tablespoons butter

Salt and pepper, to taste

Dash balsamic vinegar (optional)

Directions

Cut the stem and root ends off the onions and then slice.

Melt the butter in a large, wide, heavy pan and swirl to coat. Add the onions and stir to coat with the butter. Lower the heat to medium and let the onions cook, stirring every now and then to prevent burning. You want to let them brown but not burn. After about 30 minutes, add a little salt and pepper to taste. I also add a dash of balsamic vinegar, but that is optional.

Continue to cook and stir until the onions are a rich brown color. Store in the refrigerator tightly covered and use as desired.

Notes

These are delicious and add a gourmet touch to sandwiches, hamburgers, steak, chicken, or fish. They also add flavor to dips and spreads.

Cranberry Barbecued Chicken

SERVES 4 | PREP 10 minutes | COOK 5 hours

Ingredients

4 chicken breast halves

1 (14-ounce) can whole berry cranberry sauce

1 cup barbecue sauce (your preferred brand)

1 envelope dry onion soup mix

Directions

Place the chicken breasts in a slow cooker.

In a medium bowl, mix the cranberry sauce, barbecue sauce, and onion soup mix. Pour over the chicken. Cook on low heat in the slow cooker for 5 hours.

Notes

Serve over rice or mashed potatoes. I enjoy the leftover chicken in quesadillas or salads, as you will see in the following recipes.

Barbecued Chicken and Avocado Salad

SERVES 1 | PREP 15 minutes

Ingredients

2 cups iceberg lettuce, chopped

¼ cup Black Bean Salsa (see recipe on page 172)

4 avocado slices

4 red onion ring slices

3 tablespoons thousand island dressing (or your favorite dressing)

½ cup leftover Cranberry Barbecued Chicken (see recipe on page 175)

⅓ cup shredded Mexican cheese blend

Directions

For each salad, layer a plate with chopped iceberg lettuce. Sprinkle with the Black Bean Salsa, avocado slices, and red onion. Drizzle with your favorite dressing. For this salad I like a thousand island with jalapeno dressing. Top with leftover chicken and shredded cheese.

Notes

This recipe can be customized for whoever is eating it. This is how I like it.

Chicken Quesadilla

SERVES 2 | PREP 25 minutes | COOK 10 minutes

Ingredients

Extra virgin olive oil

4 (8-inch) flour tortillas

2 slices mozzarella cheese

1 cup leftover Cranberry Barbecue Chicken (see recipe page 175), shredded

Barbecue sauce (optional)

1 cup Monterey Jack cheese, shredded

1 tablespoon cilantro, chopped

Guacamole, salsa, and sour cream for garnish

Directions

Heat a skillet over medium heat. Brush the pan with olive oil.

Put 1 flour tortilla in the pan. Top with a slice of mozzarella cheese, half of the chicken, barbecue sauce (optional), and half of the Monterey Jack cheese. Sprinkle with half of the cilantro. Place another flour tortilla on top.

Cook until the bottom tortilla is partially browned and the cheese is partially melted. Turn and cook the other side until browned in spots and all cheese is melted. Quesadillas should be crispy on the outside and creamy on the inside.

Repeat for each quesadilla.

Serve with guacamole, salsa, and sour cream.

Notes

Macadamia Mahi Mahi

SERVES 6 | PREP 15 minutes | COOK 10 minutes

Ingredients

2 pounds mahi mahi fillets

1½ cups whole milk

¾ teaspoon salt

Dash black pepper

2 tablespoons butter

3 tablespoons all-purpose flour

1 tablespoon lemon juice

¼ cup macadamia nuts

Paprika for garnish

Directions

Place fish in a well-greased shallow baking dish.

In a bowl, combine the milk, salt, and pepper. Pour over the fish and bake at 350 degrees for 10 minutes. Remove from the oven, drain, and reserve the liquid. Keep the fish warm.

Melt the butter in a skillet. Blend in the flour, stirring constantly, and cook for 1 minute. Add the reserved liquid gradually, stirring and cooking until thickened. Stir in lemon juice.

Pour the sauce over the fish. Top with nuts and sprinkle with paprika.

Notes

Baked Salmon

SERVES 6 | PREP 20 minutes | COOK 20 minutes

Ingredients

2 tablespoons butter

1 cup brown sugar

2 tablespoons lemon juice

1 teaspoon fresh dill weed, minced

⅛ teaspoon cayenne pepper

6 center cut salmon fillets

Salt and pepper, to taste

Directions

In a small saucepan, combine the butter, brown sugar, lemon juice, dill weed, and cayenne pepper. Heat until the sugar dissolves.

Line a baking pan with foil. Place the salmon fillets on the foil. Spoon the butter mixture over each fillet. Season with additional salt and pepper if desired.

Bake at 400 degrees for about 15 minutes or until the salmon flakes with a fork.

Notes

4-Ingredient Cheese Biscuits

MAKES 2 dozen small | PREP 20 minutes | COOK 10 minutes

Ingredients

1 cup (2 sticks) butter, melted

2 cups sharp Cheddar cheese, shredded

1 cup sour cream

2 cups self-rising flour

Directions

Blend together the butter, cheese, and sour cream. Thoroughly mix in self-rising flour.

Grease a mini muffin pan. Place about 1 tablespoon of batter into each mini muffin cup.

Bake at 425 degrees for about 10 minutes or until golden.

Notes

Cheesy Garlic Bread

SERVES 4 | PREP 10 minutes | COOK 3 to 5 minutes

Ingredients

½ cup (1 stick) butter, melted

1 tablespoon garlic salt

1½ teaspoons fresh cilantro, chopped

4 thick slices French bread

4 slices mozzarella cheese (or 1 for each bread slice)

4 tablespoons Monterey Jack cheese, grated (or 1 tablespoon for each bread slice)

4 tablespoons sharp Cheddar cheese, grated (or 1 tablespoon for each bread slice)

Directions

Prepare the garlic butter by combining the butter, garlic salt, and cilantro. I keep this sealed in the refrigerator to use as needed.

For each serving, spread slices of bread with garlic butter. Top with a slice of mozzarella and 1 tablespoon of each of the grated cheeses.

Place on baking sheet and broil on low until the cheese is melted and begins to turn a little brown.

Notes

This recipe is easy to modify for however many people will be served, from one to one hundred.

Gourmet Grilled Cheese Sandwich

SERVES up to 4 | PREP 20 minutes | COOK 20 minutes

Ingredients

3 tablespoons butter, divided

1 tablespoon extra virgin olive oil

2 medium white or yellow onions, diced

1 teaspoon fresh thyme, chopped

2 teaspoons fresh rosemary, chopped and divided

Salt and pepper, to taste

1 teaspoon brown sugar

8 slices good-quality artisan bread

Mayonnaise, to taste

4 slices Gruyère cheese

4 slices white Cheddar cheese

4 slices Muenster cheese

Directions

For the caramelized onions, begin by melting 1½ tablespoons of the butter and all the olive oil in a skillet that your sandwich will fit in later. Stir in the onions, fresh thyme, and 1 teaspoon of rosemary. Season with salt and pepper. Cook over medium low heat until the onions are soft and starting to brown. Stir in the brown sugar and cook 1 more minute. Transfer the onions to a plate or bowl.

Melt the remaining butter in the skillet and stir in the remaining rosemary, swirling to coat the pan.

For each sandwich, spread one side of two pieces of bread with a little mayonnaise. Place the bread slices in the skillet, mayonnaise side down. Add a slice of each cheese to four of the bread slices and let the cheese begin to melt. Then add some of the onions. When the bread is golden and crunchy and the cheese is melted, top each cheesy slice with one of the remaining four bread slices to make a sandwich.

Notes

This recipe is easy to modify if you only need one or two sandwiches for a casual lunch. Just refrigerate the remaining caramelized onions for future use.

Zebra Crème Brûlée

SERVES 8 to 10 | PREP 30 minutes | COOK 45 minutes

Ingredients

4 cups (1 quart) heavy cream

1 quart half-and-half

1 cup sugar, divided

1 vanilla bean, halved lengthwise

14 egg yolks

Additional sugar as needed

Directions

In a medium saucepan, heat the cream and half-and-half with half of the sugar and half of the vanilla bean until steaming hot but not boiling.

Whip the remaining sugar with the yolks. Stirring constantly, add 1 teaspoon of the hot cream mixture to the yolk-sugar mixture to temper the yolks. (Tempering heats the yolks without cooking or curdling them.) Then add the tempered yolks to the pot of hot cream, stirring constantly. *Do not allow this mixture to simmer or boil.* Strain mixture through a fine mesh or tea strainer.

Divide the brûlée batter evenly among 8 to 10 ceramic ramekins (individual-serving baking dishes). Place the filled ramekins into a pan. Fill the pan with water halfway up the sides. This will keep the custard moist as it bakes. Bake at 325 degrees, uncovered, for approximately 40 minutes or until set.

Allow the cooked brûlée to rest at room temperature at least 20 minutes before caramelizing, or "brûléeing," the tops. Brûlées may be refrigerated for two days prior to serving.

To caramelize the tops before serving, place approximately 1 tablespoon of sugar on top of each brûlée. Using a torch, melt the sugar until the desired color is achieved, or place the brûlées under the preheated broiler of oven, watching closely to prevent burning.

Notes

This is one of my most-favorite desserts. The recipe comes from Jim Alexander, the extraordinary chef and owner of the wonderful restaurant Zebra, where I enjoyed fabulous food for many years.

Hot Fudge Sauce

MAKES 1½ cups | PREP 15 minutes | COOK approximately 15 minutes

Ingredients

4 tablespoons butter

2 ounces unsweetened chocolate squares

1 (12-ounce) can evaporated milk

1¼ cups sugar

½ teaspoon vanilla extract

Directions

Melt the butter and chocolate in a medium saucepan, stirring to keep from sticking. Stir in the milk and sugar. Bring to a low boil, then reduce heat and simmer until thickened, stirring often. Add the vanilla extract.

Serve over your favorite ice cream.

Notes

Leftover sauce keeps well in the refrigerator and can be microwaved when ready to serve again. I keep this in my refrigerator at all times.

Caramel Sauce

MAKES 2 cups | PREP 10 minutes | COOK 10 minutes

Ingredients

2 egg yolks

1 cup heavy cream

1 pound (16 ounces) light brown sugar

1 tablespoon butter

1 teaspoon vanilla extract

⅛ teaspoon salt

Directions

Mix egg yolks, cream, and sugar in a heavy saucepan over low heat. Cook stirring until thickened. Stir in the butter until melted and thoroughly blended into the sauce. Remove from heat and cool slightly. Stir in the vanilla extract and salt.

Notes

This sauce is delicious served over gingerbread, cake, or ice cream.

Chocolate Gravy

MAKES 1 cup | PREP 5 minutes | COOK 10 minutes

Ingredients

1 cup sugar

3 tablespoons unsweetened cocoa powder (level)

½ cup whole milk

1 tablespoon butter

½ teaspoon vanilla extract

Directions

In a medium saucepan, simmer the sugar, cocoa, and milk until thickened, about 5 to 10 minutes. Stir in the butter and vanilla until the butter is melted and well blended.

Notes

This is delicious over pound cake or other pastries. It is not for ice cream because it becomes crunchy when cold. My Hot Fudge Sauce (see recipe on page 187) is yummy over ice cream.

Ever Onward and Upward

I am often overwhelmed with gratitude for the adventures I've enjoyed and the people I've enjoyed them with. I know I still have lots of great adventures ahead of me too!

Reflections

Living My Best Life 192
Adversity Can Be Your Friend 194
Friends, Faith, and Fortitude 196
See You in Heaven 199
Age Gracefully 208
What's Next? 212

Living My Best Life

While I am still very involved in several business projects, the best part of my life these days is focusing on the joy of my family and friends while being grateful for an interesting, fulfilling life that brought me to this peaceful, happy place.

I spend my happiest times with my children and grandchildren, seeing them succeed and thrive. We have been a bonded trio all these decades, always looking out for each other. Yes, I had a very busy career, but I immersed myself in their activities with all the gratitude that I could. Everything I had the privilege of doing with them was a joy. They

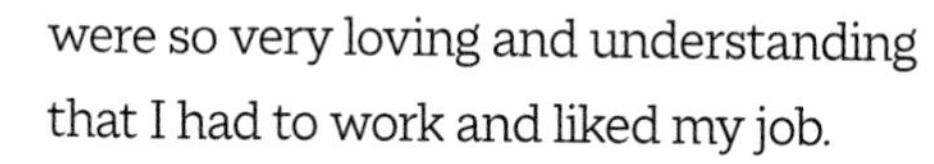

were so very loving and understanding that I had to work and liked my job.

I was thankful that my employer allowed me to work flexible hours even though this was at a time before women with children were fully accepted in the workforce. I was the only mom who worked outside the home among Michael's Cub Scout troop, but I eagerly became their scout leader. I still have

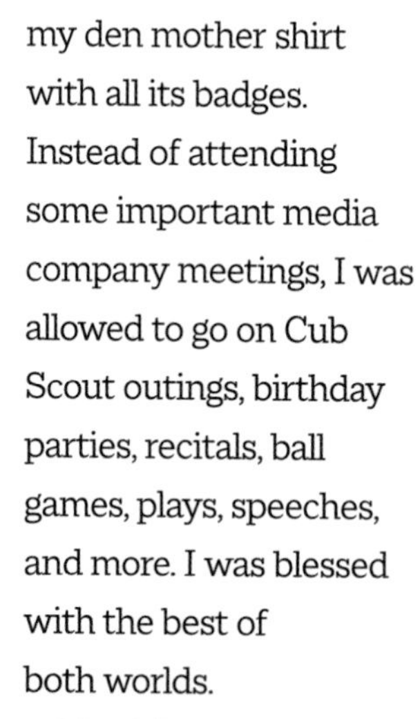

my den mother shirt with all its badges. Instead of attending some important media company meetings, I was allowed to go on Cub Scout outings, birthday parties, recitals, ball games, plays, speeches, and more. I was blessed with the best of both worlds.

My children were always so patient when

they had to go places with me when they may have preferred playing in the yard with friends. They went to the grocery store, the hair salon, the TV studio, and on work trips aboard planes and ships. They met a lot of interesting people. As a result, they have no fear of crowds, public speaking, or cameras. From an early age, they could perform or carry on a conversation with a stranger or a superstar, totally at ease and unimpressed. They appeared with me in person and on camera. My coworkers and viewers watched them grow up with me and still ask about them. But my favorite times were the simple things like tucking them in bed at night, hearing about their day, and driving them to school. Michael was younger, so he had more time going to work with me and with me driving him to school. I was sad when he turned sixteen and could drive himself. I still miss those simple but profoundly special times.

I have so many wonderful memories of our adventures together. And now, after doing my best to take care of them, they are definitely taking care of me. They are generous, caring, and loving in every way. We continue our adventures, but this time I go with them. We live in three different states, but the three of us remain as close as ever.

Among the many lessons I learned and wish I had known from the start is that adversity can be your friend.

Adversity Can Be Your Friend

You learn important life lessons far better during adversity than through the happy, easy times. I experienced some challenging times during this phase of my life. I am so happy to be back in action after a crazy 2018, from start to finish.

On January 11, 2018, I was out "power walking" at night (don't do that) and tripped on a piece of broken sidewalk. I lacerated my face and broke my jaw on both sides. I don't know how one can do that much damage just by tripping, but I did. After six hours in the emergency room, they stitched up my face and sent me home saying that nothing could be done about the broken bones until the swelling was reduced, maybe in six days. During that time, the bones in my jaws separated even more.

I was in agony when my dentist for decades, Dr. Ross Nash, called and said, "You need help *now,* and I know the best oral and facial surgeon in the world. May I call him for you?" Dr. Nash is not only an amazing cosmetic dentist known all over the world for his work, but he is an amazing friend. He called Dr. Raymond Haigney, who went to the hospital after his long day, looked at my X-rays, and was shocked at what he saw. Dr. Haigney sent a car for me immediately to take me to the hospital. He did emergency surgery, which required a huge incision, rebreaking my jaw, moving nerves, and putting me back together with plates, screws, and even more stitches than Carrie Underwood had from her accident. Dr. Haigney and Dr. Nash are talented, caring, and dedicated. After three months of partial facial paralysis and lots of prayers, everything miraculously healed. I am completely back to normal. My teeth kept shifting during this ordeal, but Dr. Nash got those back together. Praise God, I am very blessed with great doctors.

One week after my face and mouth surgery, I heard back from my mammogram that had been done before my accident. I had breast cancer. Dr. Peter Turk, another talented doctor, was assigned to my case. I learned that he is one of the best in the country. After surgery and radiation, I am completely cancer-free and confident that I experienced yet another miracle.

That was followed by a painful bout of pneumonia, small skin cancer, and the death of my beloved cat of fourteen years. It was quite a year, but I can honestly say that through it all, by the grace of God, I knew everything would be just fine. I look back and never feel bitter, only *better* and grateful for the life lessons I learned and the many who prayed for me, like Rhonda, Beth, Kelly, Patti, James, Loran, Sandra, and Kim, and organizations around the world prayed at the request of special friends.

It is with such gratitude that I can get back to doing things I love and spending time with the people I love.

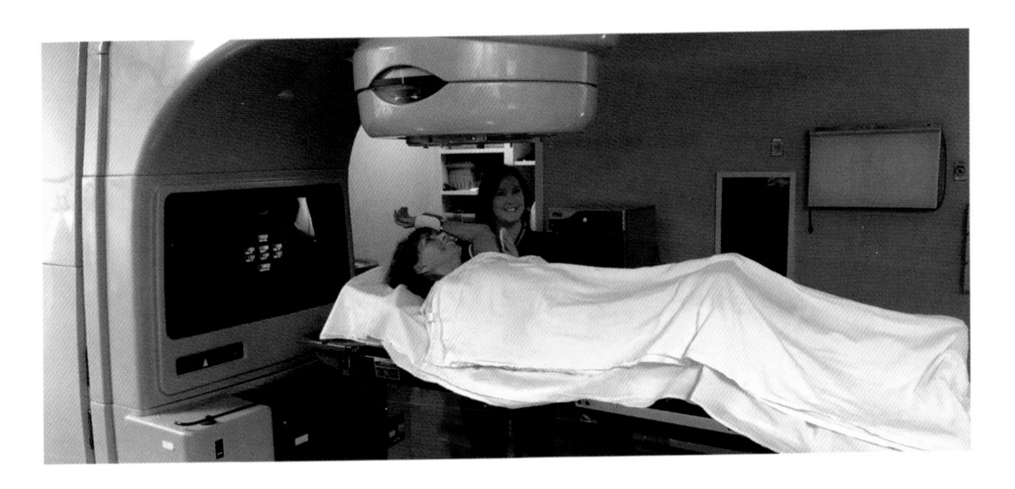

You learn important life lessons far better during adversity than through the happy, easy times.

Friends, Faith, and Fortitude

An important part of my aging gracefully is being surrounded by supportive friends who have encouraged me, tolerated me, and accepted me unconditionally. Studies show that good friends make us healthier and happier. I am thankful for so many and grateful for each one.

My wonderful friends have taught me how to be a better friend. They are in cities around the world. Some are famous; most are not. Some I've known for decades; some are new but became instant soulmates. As you get older, you recognize the important qualities right away. Good friends want things *for* you, not *from* you. I hope each and every one of you whom I am blessed to have as a friend know that I love you, appreciate you, and smile every time I think of you. You know who you are. You know how you have touched my life and how much I treasure you.

I am often asked how I have such comfortable conversations with strangers and make friends so easily. It comes so naturally that I have to stop and think about why that is. As I described in my story about meeting Elvis as a child, I mentioned that my father knew no strangers. As a child and teenager, it used to drive me a little crazy because wherever we went, he ended up talking to every person along the way for a long time. He cared about and respected all kinds of people.

I seem to have inherited that. It's a quality that was very helpful in my job of interviewing about twenty-five strangers each week on live TV for decades. When not on TV, that quality makes meeting and chatting with new people easy and

I hope each and every one of you whom I am blessed to have as a friend know that I love you, appreciate you, and smile every time I think of you. You know who you are. You know how you have touched my life and how much I treasure you.

fun, especially without three television cameras surrounding me. I simply find out what they like to talk about and let them know I genuinely want to listen to what they have to say. Then I respond with things we have in common. Then acquaintances become special friends. That is true whether the person is a newsmaker or a movie star or a new neighbor. We are all just people who appreciate kindness, thoughtfulness, and understanding. I've been blessed with wonderful friends from all walks of life and I am grateful for each unique friendship.

Another recurring question in my life has been, "How do you stay so perky and happy all the time?" We all have highs and lows in our complicated lives. It's how you respond to them that makes a difference. Fortunately, I have been rooted and grounded in faith and love from the beginning of my life. In difficult times, I don't dwell on how bad things are. I put my focus on the blessings. No matter what our situation, there is still goodness and joy. I thank God for those things and ask for His help with the rest.

From reading this book, you know I have not been spared from difficult times. Truthfully, I did not go into detail about the scariest, most disheartening, saddest challenges of my life because

that is not what I dwell on. Believe it or not, I have learned to thank God for the adversities because those dark times have always brought positive, wonderful changes that I would have never known otherwise.

This life is so very brief. The older I get, the more I realize that, good or bad, this too shall pass. So I focus on the blessings. Focus on the positive things we too often take for granted.

I know it all sounds so "Pollyanna-like," but trust me—it works. I begin every day before I get out of bed with, "Thank you, God. I have another day to enjoy. I can hardly wait to see what You have in store for me. Give me the wisdom and protection to manage it all."

When you begin each day with praise and gratitude, good things happen, and you notice them. You know you have help with the challenges. God has rewarded my faithfulness and belief. I am truly blessed and favored because I trust, I believe, and I show gratitude, no matter the circumstances. It keeps me smiling and happy.

Fortunately, I have been rooted and grounded in faith and love from the beginning of my life. In difficult times, I don't dwell on how bad things are. I put my focus on the blessings.

See You in Heaven

As we age, losing precious loved ones is a reminder of our own mortality. I have no symptoms or signs that I will be seeing anyone in heaven real soon, but my experiences assure me that I will see all of my Christian family and friends there one day. And, yes, my pets too because God takes care of them as He does all His innocent creations.

I have shared the following stories with a few people who suggested that I write about them in hopes of bringing comfort and peace to others. I don't know why these things have happened to me, but I wonder if it's because I asked for signs and believed I would receive them.

The Day My Mom Went to Heaven

I grew up in a family who read and believed the Bible. Sure, we had fun, sometimes maybe too much, but we always lived each day with praises and pleas, praying through the ups and downs of life.

The day after Thanksgiving a few years ago, I awoke with an urgency to visit my mom who lived an hour away. My children were home, and they had traveled from a few states away for the holiday. I also had appointments and activities scheduled. My mom had been sick for over a decade with Alzheimer's. She was at the heartbreaking stage of not even recognizing me, so logic would say that I could wait until Sunday to race off to see her when my children were not there and things weren't so hectic. But I felt compelled to go *right then*.

As I drove over, I braced myself for another sad visit. For the past few years, my once-beautiful mom looked so fearful and frightened, not knowing my name or being able to sit up or communicate. But to my shock, she was sitting up and glowing. She looked the way I had not seen her in years. She greeted me with recognition and excitement, "I am so happy that you are here. I love you." We conversed in ways we had not in years. My brother, David, was there as well, which was also unusual because we were rarely there at the same time. We both just stared in confusion but with gratitude. I was also glad David was there to witness this with me.

She greeted me with recognition and excitement, "I am so happy that you are here. I love you."

We called the caregiver in and asked if our mom was on new drugs, looking for a practical, earthly reason for all this. The kind nurse said emphatically, "No, she just started this early this morning."

My mom began to communicate in interesting ways. She looked around the room greeting beings that we could not see and whom she had not seen in a very long time. She greeted them, smiling and glowing and happy. It was joyful and riveting to see. She looked at us and clearly declared with a huge smile, "*This is delightful.*"

I needed to get back to my children and responsibilities at home. I kissed my mom and said what I often said as I left, "We will see each other in heaven someday." This time she smiled and nodded.

Several hours later, I received a call saying my mom had passed away. How grateful I will always be to have seen her on the way to heaven and have the assurance that all we have been taught and believed is true. I don't know why I was given this gift. Maybe it's because He knew I would share it.

My Daddy Goes to Heaven

I had a very similar situation with my daddy. He was on a fishing trip in Alaska to bring back more of the halibut we all loved. It was his favorite pastime. Unfortunately, he collapsed and was rushed back home where it was determined that he had advanced lung cancer and a short time to live. Along with losing my dad, I was very concerned about his eternity. He was such a good man, but I was not so sure he was a saved man.

He was in the hospital in lots of pain. I tiptoed in, and he gave me a big smile. It was just the two of us. Suddenly, he grabbed his chest in pain, but this time instead of exclaiming words that I cannot write here, he began praying. It was the most beautiful, sincere prayer. He sounded like Billy Graham. I was stunned and grateful, but shocked. When he finished, I quietly asked if he was OK. He quickly responded, "I am now."

His pain seemed to disappear. He then told me that an evangelist from Europe came to visit him in the hospital and prepared him for going to heaven. It was a beautiful story, but it seemed odd for so many reasons. I later asked the nurses, my mom, and my brother about this mysterious woman. No one knew of any woman of this description visiting him. I believe she was an angel.

Daddy lived a few more weeks, but he was in a coma and could not communicate. I had to go back to work since no one really knew when Daddy might head to heaven. As a part of my job, I needed to go to Florida to do my show live from Disney World. I always took my children on those trips. Elizabeth, Michael, and I were in the parking lot of WBTV on our way to the airport when someone shouted to me that I needed to come back in for a phone call. I was told that my daddy was hanging on and they were sure he would not go until I was present. I certainly did not want him to suffer.

He sounded like Billy Graham. I was stunned and grateful, but shocked.

My children and I took off to my hometown of Shelby instead of Disney World. We surrounded Daddy's bed. Suddenly, Daddy began to slightly smile and just glowed with a look of joy. The wonderful hospice nurse asked him quietly, "Archie, do you see Jesus and your family?" My father who was too weak to lift a finger moments before, then lifted his entire arm and stretched his hand powerfully toward the sky with a nod and huge grin on his face as if he was reaching out to grip another outstretched hand. I will never ever forget that, and neither will my children.

I mentioned pets going to heaven. I've also had such comforting, reassuring, similar experiences with them. I know that many of you understand that loss as being as profoundly difficult as human loved ones. I hope my next stories make you smile.

My Pet Peeve

I bet you thought I was about to grumble about something, didn't you? Actually my pet Peeve was a joy in my life. Peeve was an orange tabby cat who adopted me. He just showed up at my house one day and took over. As far as cats go, Peeve was a bit of a curmudgeon, but underneath it all, he was a loving little creature who especially liked to make me laugh when I didn't feel much like it and snuggled up especially close when I was sick. He did something to make me happy every day of his sixteen years on this earth.

It was a very sad week when Peeve passed away, but it was also a week of hope and enlightenment, which is why I share this story.

Peeve had become so ill with the many ailments that come to cats who live so long. I selfishly wanted him to hang in there, but on a busy weekday morning, I knew I needed to take him to the vet, hoping they would give him some magic potion to make him feel better. For the first time ever, Peeve did not "argue" with me about going to the vet, a place where he unfortunately held a record for being the most-difficult cat to give a physical. But not on this day. He seemed to welcome Dr. Killough's gentle touch, but I did not welcome the good doctor's bad news that it was "time."

The day had come for me to make such a big decision, and I really wasn't prepared for that news. Peeve pushed his way over to me and put his head up to mine, forehead to forehead, as if to say, "Please help me." We stayed that way for about two minutes. It was odd, but it gave me the strength to say, "I understand." We said our goodbyes. I held Peeve in my arms and watched the light in his big orange eyes go out and felt the breath go out of me. This was not how my day was supposed to start.

To make it even worse, I had to pull myself together and do *nine* on-camera TV commercials that day. When I dragged myself home that Friday night, I began sobbing nonstop for over twenty-four hours. During that time, my children called to see how I was doing. My son commented that probably what I would miss most were the times that Peeve, no matter what, plopped in the middle of my newspaper when I was trying to read it, then get up meowing loudly to go out. As soon as I would let him out and sit back down, he would flop himself on the doormat and "yell" to come back in. We did this little routine every day, and I'm sure Peeve was snickering each time at how well he had me trained—up and down trying to read the paper.

Peeve was a bit of a curmudgeon, but underneath it all, he was a loving little creature who especially liked to make me laugh.

On Sunday morning after Peeve's passing, I was lying in bed praying, asking God to give me a sign that I made the right decision about Peeve and that Peeve really was in heaven. I told God that this was not a question of faith but of comfort, and if He didn't have time to show me a sign, I would understand. I then walked downstairs to witness something very extraordinary. My newest cat, Grey, stared at me intensely as I entered the kitchen. He then leaped up on my newspaper with the same quirky motions of Peeve. The moment I slowly sat down, Grey bolted for the door meowing all the way. I opened the door in slow motion, and Grey ran outside and flopped on the mat "yelling" to come back in. Grey has done that little routine that one and only time, never before and never since. I had my sign, and I know God winked.

She was the cat who stood by me and comforted me as I saw my children leave the nest and begin their own lives. Many of you know the feeling of transferring your nurturing need to be a mother from your children to your pets. That was Miu.

My Constant Companion Miu

Miu was my quiet, ladylike cat who rarely made a sound and never attracted attention with anything but her beauty, sweetness, and intense loyalty to me. For all of her eighteen years and forty-five days on earth, she rarely left my side. She curled up by my computer, stood watch while I cooked, slept on my bed, and somehow knew I needed her nearby all the time.

She was the cat who stood by me and comforted me as I saw my children leave the nest and begin their own lives. Many of you know the feeling of transferring your nurturing need to be a mother from your children to your pets. That was Miu. She knew I needed her, and she was there. I had been the only mother she knew from the time she was abandoned in my neighbor's garage. Her feline mother gave birth and took off. I cared for Miu from the time she fit in the palm of my hand only a few days old, until she went to heaven more than eighteen years later.

Miu went through some name changes until I renamed her for Miuccia Prada, a favorite designer. That one stuck because Miu was elegant, walked like a model, and had a gorgeous fur coat. We had many wonderful "conversations." I talked while every now and then she would make a little leap into the air with a chirping sound, as if to say, "I know ... right?" That was about the only sound she ever made. She would wind around my legs letting me know she was there for me and loved me.

She also had a special relationship with Mike. When he would begin preparing for his radio show in the middle of the night while everyone else was sleeping, Miu would appear and go through several nightly rituals and see him off to work before heading back to her duty to look after me.

One day after many healthy, happy years Miu got sick. We tried hard to save her with all kinds of medical procedures but knew her time on earth was up. Her work was done. My son, Michael, came home to be with Miu and me for her last hours. As many of you know, it is like losing a precious family member. As with my other cats, I prayed for and received signs that Miu was well and happy in heaven. To this day, I hear her little chirp at the most unexpected times. The most astonishing sign is when I am at my desk and feel a furry feline swirling around my feet. I quickly look, expecting a current cat, yet no one is visible. I was startled and confused when this first began, but now I smile and know it's a visit from Miu.

My Amazing Grey

Grey was my most entertaining cat. He was a determined, loving, playful, smart, cantankerous, loyal cat with an amazing personality that kept me laughing. He came into my life demonstrating his tenacity and strong will from the start. I was at my storage unit unloading 30,000 pounds of my magazines with help of some workers. Truthfully, I sat on the curb and watched as they worked. Suddenly, a precious little gray and white kitty jumped onto my lap and began purring. I knew I could not keep him. I already had two jealous cats. One of my helpers picked him up and placed him over the fence of the buildings to keep him out of the way. This little gray kitten dug his way back under the fence three times, each time hopping onto my lap. How could I resist? I decided to help him find a home. Long story short, I fell in love with this feisty little ball of fluff, named him Grey, and he instantly made himself right at home with me.

There are many very funny stories about Grey, but I will skip to the end to share how, yet again, God confirmed for me that my loved ones will be waiting for me in heaven, people and animals. At the age of ten human years, Grey got cancer. My wonderful vet, Dr. Richard Killough, knew I was not ready to give Grey up

He came into my life demonstrating his tenacity and strong will from the start.

and suggested chemo. I had to pray about that because I did not want Grey to suffer. The answer was to try and see how he handled it. Grey took on chemo like a champ. He was stoic and never let on that it was a problem. He loved his life. He stopped sleeping on my bed but seemed very comfortable curled up nearby. Grey became quite well known at Long Animal Hospital and received cheers every month as he marched in for his treatment. He holds the record as the cat to survive the longest on chemo—three years.

Two years into Grey's monthly treatments, I had my accident and then got my cancer diagnosis. As soon as Grey realized I had been hurt and was sick, he jumped back up on my very tall bed and slept with his head on my pillow every night. During the night, he would check on me with his nose on my face, I suppose to make sure I was still breathing.

Thankfully, I healed from the accident, two surgeries, and radiation for six weeks. I was all well. Grey apparently felt like his work was done and decided he was ready to go. After three years of monthly chemo, he stopped eating and drinking. I would carry him outside to his favorite sunny spot next to my pond. He and my fish had a special relationship and continued to communicate to the end.

I was devastated to lose my precious companion. I sat alone by my pond and prayed for a sign to let me know that Grey made it to heaven. Since I was especially sad this time, God sent me two big signs. I looked up, and there were clouds in the clear blue sky in the perfect shape of a cat—head, ears, and long body with a tail standing straight up. I have never seen anything like it. Then a dragonfly appeared hovering over my pond. I had never seen one there before. This dragonfly stayed for days and followed me.

During that time, the grandchildren of a dear friend of mine came to visit and feed my fish. They were fascinated and delighted watching the dragonfly follow me around. One of them asked, "What about your other two cats that went to heaven? Have they come to visit?" As I was explaining that it seemed to just be Grey, two more dragonflies suddenly appeared. The three of them hovered together. The children and I were speechless. Then we laughed and thanked God for such precious moments.

The dragonflies left after a week and none have ever returned in three years. I had my signs, and I know Grey will be ready to jump in my lap the moment I arrive in heaven.

I am betting that many of you have had similar experiences and miss and love your furry family members the way I do. If you have lost a dear pet or lose one in the future, please find comfort in these little stories. They left me assured that animals go to heaven. We just have to make sure we know how to get there to see them again.

If you have lost a dear pet or lose one in the future, please find comfort in these little stories. They left me assured that animals go to heaven. We just have to make sure we know how to get there to see them again.

Age Gracefully

It's hard for me to grasp that I have seen my seventieth birthday. In my head, I'm about thirty-five—but not in my mirror. I have some good genes and the desire to keep myself in the best shape possible, especially after my reminder that it can all change in a moment. An attitude of gratitude and the promise that I will do my part to stay healthy and look the best I can have made a huge difference in the aging process for me.

The question that many may be curious about and want to ask is whether I have had plastic surgery. It used to be so taboo. When I was in my thirties and very busy doing multiple TV shows and all things related to that, the subject came up between a coworker and me. At that young age, I was very cavalier and dismissive about it. When I replied that I don't know if I would or not,

Photo and Styling By: Kate Lee

she told me, "Rumor has it that you have had everything done from head to toe." That left me speechless and shocked. But then I thought that if I ever wanted plastic surgery, then why not since people had already decided that I had. Thankfully, maturity has taught me to never base any decision on what other people think since many of them make up their own narratives and scenarios that have nothing to do with me.

So now that I am several decades older, the answer to that question is, *yes*, I have had plastic surgery, and I've had it recently. It was a prayerful decision based on research and what I want for myself, not what anyone else might think. Cosmetic surgery has become far more accessible, affordable, and popular. For me, it wasn't to look younger or erase years, but it was to look refreshed, rested, and healthy. Those qualities encourage me to match them with more exercise, a better diet, and a more positive outlook. I definitely did not want drama or change. I just wanted a few subtle tweaks. If I can look and feel my best and take care of this body God gave me, then why would I not?

An essential consideration for plastic surgery is choosing the right doctor. I want a doctor who is safe, talented, experienced, very skillful, thoughtful, respectful of my wishes, and who shares my faith. My plastic surgeons were first Dr. Peter Tucker and now Dr. Robert Graper. Both are as kind and caring as they are extraordinarily talented at what they do. Recently, Dr. Graper asked my goals and what procedures I thought I wanted. After listening carefully, he examined me to assess what would be realistic and attainable, based on his experience from performing many thousands of successful surgeries and his extraordinary skill. I am thrilled that he delivered just what I wanted—to look refreshed and healthy, nothing dramatic.

It's very important to note that while plastic surgery and skin care can be excellent, safe solutions to slow the appearance of the aging process, they are far from the most important. Staying young at heart is what really turns back the clock. Forget about acting your age. Just act yourself and enjoy each day. A youthful heart is contagious.

What are a few of my most effective ways of staying young and loving life? One of the most important bits of advice I can share for aging gracefully is to find the best primary care doctor for *you*. Of course, you want a brilliant doctor, but equally important is that they are caring, compassionate, and became a doctor for the right reason—to help people. You want someone who knows your name, not just a number and time slot, and genuinely cares about your well-being. I met my doctor in another one of those "meant to be" moments. I was sick and made an appointment with my usual primary MD. When I arrived, I was told that he was away and another doctor was filling in that day. That's how I met the doctor who immediately said to me, "I will take care of you as I would my own mother," and he has done that since meeting him that day many years ago. His practice is quite a distance from where I live, but I gladly make the drive to see Dr. Steven Gilchrist. Look for that kind of doctor.

I also smile and laugh a lot. I choose to be surrounded by positive, fun, uplifting people who make me laugh and who share the same appreciation and zest for life that I have. Life is too short to spend time with anyone whose spirit does not lift yours. That doesn't mean everyone has to be happy all the time. There are sad times, and those can be especially meaningful with people you consider kindred spirits. It is gratifying to help a friend through a tough time and vice versa.

I dress youthfully because it makes me happy. As long as I am tasteful and respectful of those around me, I will continue to wear the things that make me cheerful. Some days, it's colorful classics with a twist that are sometimes a little whimsical. Other days I want rich, dark colors that are still soft, feminine,

romantic, and pretty. Occasionally, I will choose a theme while being careful not to look like I'm in a costume. I often start with a pair of shoes or a handbag or a pair of earrings and build from there. We all have to get dressed, so why not make it fun and enjoy it all day.

Countless times I have been told by strangers as I just go about the mundane tasks of life—grocery store, outdoors for walks, shopping at a garden center, standing in a post office line, taking my cat to the vet—that my outfit brightened their day. That brightens mine. People genuinely appreciate others who make an effort to make every moment special. My goal is to make at least one person smile and feel happy every day. I am spontaneous, present, and never afraid to laugh at myself. Humility comes easy for me.

I adore my family. I enjoy my life, their lives, and our time together. If we are not enjoying our own lives, no one is going to enjoy *us*. I love spending time with my grandchildren. Their enthusiasm and exuberance for fun keep *my* life fun. I show up ready to do whatever they choose. Embrace those moments. Live through your children and grandchildren without telling them how to live.

I never stop hoping, dreaming, and wishfully thinking. I thrive on thinking about possibilities and opportunities.

Those things make each day more fun, keep a smile on my face, and give me my "never-give-up" attitude. That has gotten me through some rough times.

And of course, I will always enjoy good food and never deny myself things I love—desserts, all things chocolate, real butter, real whipped cream, fried chicken, milkshakes, Krispy Kreme, soul food, french fries, and so much more. The secret is *moderation*. I try to eat more healthy food than "junk food," and I'm mindful of everything I consume, but I will not deny myself yummy food. It's responsible for so much happiness and joy in my life, as well as this book.

What's Next?

How grateful I am for an interesting life of faith, food, media, fun with friends, and the joy of my wonderful family. But I am not done. I will never just mark time and let the clock run out. I will never lose my childlike excitement for what each new day may bring. I plan to live each day to its fullest. I am certain that I still have new adventures ahead. I'm sure there will be trials too, but as a favorite minister has said, "Let your trials prove the authenticity of your faith ... and persevere."

Thank you for reading my book. It happened because of my wonderful children, grandchildren, *and you.*

Be blessed in all you do. Love life and enjoy delicious food every day.

Friends and Family Favorite Recipes

One of my greatest joys in life is feeding my family and friends. These are a few of their favorite recipes. Visit my blog at BarbaraMcKay.com and tell me your favorite!

Elizabeth's Spinach Dip 214
Margaret's Bacon Buttery Bites 215
Sweet and Spicy Roasted Pecans 216
Lemon Nutmeg Scones 217
Linda's Chicken and Vegetable Soup 218
Watermelon Mango Salad 220
Holiday Rosemary Grapefruit 222
Spring Green Salad with Berries and Avocado 223
Michael's Red Chicken 224
Michael's White Chicken 225
Bloomin' Onion Quiche with Goat Cheese and Thyme 226
Crispy Baked Parmesan Chicken 228
Barbecued Meatloaf 229
Elizabeth's Creamy Gruyère Chicken 230
Slow-Cooked Barbecued Pork Tenderloin 233
Make-Ahead Sausage and Egg Casserole 234
Fresh Shrimp Salad 235
Roasted Brussels Sprouts 236
Gingered Asparagus with Cashews 237
Broccoli Salad 238
Tomato Cheese Pie 239
Cheese Grits 240
Elizabeth's Mac and Cheese 241
Almond Joy Cake 242
Chocolate Chess Pie 243
Annette's Brownies 244
DeDe's Messy Pie 246
OREO Cookie Freeze 248
Perfect Pecan Pie 249
Pink Things 250
My Favorite Rum Cake 251
Special Day Dessert 253
Troutman Pound Cake and Teddy Bears 254
Smoothies 257
Ultimate Cheesecake 258
Rita's Baked Apple Pie Shake 259

Elizabeth's Spinach Dip

MAKES 3 cups | PREP 30 minutes

Ingredients

1 large purple cabbage

½ cup mayonnaise

1⅓ cups sour cream

1 (8-ounce) can water chestnuts, drained and chopped

⅓ cup green onion, sliced

1 teaspoon lemon juice

¾ teaspoon seasoned salt

½ teaspoon dried dill weed

1 (10-ounce) package frozen chopped spinach, thawed and drained

Crackers and fresh vegetables of your choice

Directions

Slice off the core end of the red cabbage to form a flat base. Fold back several outer leaves. Cut a crosswise slice from top of cabbage. Cut out enough of inner part to form a bowl for the dip. Set aside.

In a mixing bowl, blend the mayonnaise and sour cream. Stir in water chestnuts, green onions, lemon juice, salt, and dill weed. Squeeze excess moisture from the spinach and add to dip.

At serving time, spoon the dip into the cabbage bowl. Serve with crackers and fresh vegetables.

Notes

It is so much fun for me to learn about new and delicious recipes from my daughter, Elizabeth. She has served on many cookbook committees and provided great recipes for Atlanta-area cookbooks. I'm so proud to have some of her favorites in my book.

Margaret's Bacon Buttery Bites

SERVES 30 | PREP 20 minutes | COOK 45 minutes

Ingredients

30 Ritz crackers

12 slices of thin bacon, cut into thirds

¾ cup light brown sugar

Directions

Place a piece of the bacon on top of each cracker. Add a teaspoon of brown sugar.

Line a few rimmed baking sheets with foil. Arrange each cracker appetizer on the foil.

Bake at a low 250 degrees until the bacon is cooked and glazed. Drain before serving.

Notes

This fun and delicious recipe is from my daughter's sister-in-law, Margaret Lesley, who is married to my son-in-law's twin. I am so thankful for Margaret who lives around the corner from Elizabeth and Brett in Atlanta. I can always count on kind, thoughtful Margaret to be there for my family. In fact, she took Elizabeth to the hospital to give birth to my second grandchild, who came surprisingly early while both Brett and I were out of town. Margaret is a joy and never misses an opportunity to brighten my world.

Sweet and Spicy Roasted Pecans

MAKES 3 cups | PREP 20 minutes | COOK 25 minutes

Ingredients

2 tablespoons butter

½ cup brown sugar

½ teaspoon cayenne pepper

1 teaspoon cinnamon

Fine sea salt, to taste

3 cups large pecan halves

Directions

Melt the butter in a large skillet. Stir in the brown sugar, cayenne pepper, and cinnamon. Cook and stir until sugar melts. Add pecans to skillet and stir until coated.

Spread pecans on a foil-covered rimmed baking sheet. Sprinkle with salt to taste.

Bake at a low 300 degrees for about 25 minutes or until lightly browned and fragrant.

Notes

Lemon Nutmeg Scones

SERVES 8 | PREP 15 minutes | COOK 15 minutes

Ingredients

1¾ cups all-purpose flour

¼ cup cornstarch

¼ cup sugar

1 teaspoon baking soda

¼ teaspoon nutmeg

6 tablespoons butter

8 ounces lemon yogurt, divided

2 eggs, beaten

2 tablespoons sugar

⅛ teaspoon nutmeg

3 ounces cream cheese, softened

Directions

Combine flour, cornstarch, the ¼ cup of sugar, baking soda, and the ¼ teaspoon of nutmeg. Mix well. Cut in the butter using a pastry cutter or food processor.

Stir in half of the lemon yogurt and all the eggs. Mix just until moistened, being careful not to overbeat.

Shape the sticky dough into a ball on a floured surface. Press into a 9-inch circle on a greased baking sheet.

Combine remaining sugar and nutmeg. Sprinkle over the dough. Cut into wedges and place on a baking sheet at least 1 inch apart. Bake at 425 degrees until light brown, about 12 to 15 minutes.

Mix the cream cheese with the remaining lemon yogurt.

Serve scones with a dollop of the lemon cream on top. Blueberries are also a delicious addition to the batter before baking.

Notes

I wanted to include a recipe in honor of my special English friend Earl Charles Spencer. Many a scone has been served at his Althorp home, a magical place that my daughter Elizabeth and I loved visiting as his guests.

Linda's Chicken and Vegetable Soup

SERVES 8 | PREP 20 minutes | COOK 1 hour

Ingredients

4 boneless, skinless chicken breasts

Salt and pepper, to taste

2 handfuls of fresh green beans

2 cups frozen lima beans

4 medium potatoes, diced

2 medium onions, chopped

2 (10-ounce) cans tomato soup

1 (28-ounce) can diced tomatoes

1 (15-ounce) can white corn

1 (8-ounce) can yellow corn

1 (10-ounce) can chicken broth

1 (10-ounce) can beef broth

Directions

Place the chicken breasts in a large soup pot and cover with water. Season with salt and pepper. Cover and simmer until done, about 25 minutes. Remove the chicken from the pot and save the liquid in the pot. Chop the chicken into bite-size pieces and return it to the pot with the liquid.

Add the fresh green beans, lima beans, potatoes, and onions. Simmer for 20 minutes. Let cool for 20 minutes. Add the tomato soup, diced tomatoes, white corn, yellow corn, chicken broth, and beef broth. Simmer 20 minutes more. Season with additional salt and pepper if desired.

Serve warm.

Notes

Linda Hendrick is NASCAR royalty. To me, she is an extraordinary friend. We have traveled together in cars, planes, and beautiful ships. Our daughters grew up together and were in each other's weddings. There are precious and funny memories of our sons as little boys growing up together. We have celebrated victories and cried over huge heartaches together. Through it all, she has been a powerful influence on my faith walk by her shining example.

Watermelon Mango Salad

SERVES 4 | PREP 30 minutes

Ingredients

2 cups seedless watermelon, cut into bite-size chunks

2 mangos, peeled and cut into chunks

½ cup cucumbers, thinly sliced

½ cup red onion, finely sliced

½ cup cherry tomatoes, sliced

1 tablespoon pickled jalapeno peppers, chopped

1 cup fresh spinach leaves

Dressing:

2 tablespoons lemon juice

1 tablespoon extra virgin olive oil

1 tablespoon honey

1 teaspoon garlic, minced

½ teaspoon salt

3 tablespoons fresh cilantro, chopped

Feta or goat cheese, to taste (optional)

Directions

In a large bowl, toss together all the salad in ingredients, including the watermelon, mangos, cucumbers, onion, tomatoes, peppers, and spinach.

Prepare the dressing by combining the lemon juice, olive oil, honey, garlic, salt, and cilantro and whisking to mix thoroughly. Toss the dressing with the fruits and vegetables.

Optionally, top with feta or goat cheese.

Notes

For decades I have visited Simpson's Produce on Kings Drive in Charlotte at least once or twice a week. It is the best, and so are the people who work there. They have been special friends since my early TV days and continue to provide the most delicious fruit, vegetables, and shopping experience from April to October. After that, they provide our fall pumpkins and then our fresh Christmas trees. The market is owned by third-generation Simpsons, David and Norman. Tragically, David lost his life in 2020 to COVID-19 complications. His friendly, kind face will be missed by all. I think of him as I make this recipe because his father, Darryl Simpson, called David the watermelon savant. He and Ronnie at the watermelon tent knew how to pick out the sweetest and juiciest from the mountain of watermelons they offer. You will still find Ronnie there ready to help and missing David's smiling face like the rest of us. Thank you, David, Norman, and Ronnie. Those watermelons you chose for me were perfect every time, and I know Ronnie will continue in David's memory.

Holiday Rosemary Grapefruit

SERVES 8 | PREP 20 minutes | COOK 15 minutes

Ingredients

¾ cup water

1½ cups sugar

4 tablespoons honey

4 sprigs fresh rosemary

1 (64-ounce) container grapefruit sections

1 small (10-ounce) jar maraschino cherries (no stems)

Directions

Combine the water, sugar, honey, and rosemary in a saucepan. Bring to a boil over medium heat. Simmer 5 minutes. Remove from heat and cool for about 15 minutes.

Drain the grapefruit sections and cherries and place in a glass bowl. Pour the rosemary syrup over the fruit. Chill until ready to serve.

Notes

This is an all-time friends and family favorite. It is a staple on our holiday brunch menu along with the Make-Ahead Sausage and Egg Casserole (page 234), Cheese Grits (page 240), and packaged sweet rolls. I usually buy Sister Schubert's Cinnamon Rolls. I also keep it in my refrigerator as often as possible as a quick lunch side dish with a favorite sandwich or soup.

Spring Green Salad with Berries and Avocado

SERVES 4 | PREP 20 minutes

Ingredients

1 head of Boston lettuce, torn into bite-size pieces

12 strawberries, sliced

3 kiwis, peeled and sliced

1 avocado, peeled, pitted, and cubed or sliced

Goat cheese, crumbled (optional)

Glazed walnuts or pecans (optional)

Orange dressing (below)

Dressing:

3 tablespoons raspberry vinegar

⅓ cup extra virgin olive oil

3 tablespoons fresh orange juice

½ teaspoon salt

⅛ teaspoon black pepper

Directions

Toss together the lettuce, strawberries, and kiwi. Add the avocado just before serving to preserve its color. Toss with the dressing. Add goat cheese and glazed walnuts or pecans if desired.

For the dressings, whisk together the vinegar, olive oil, orange juice, salt, and pepper until mixed well.

Notes

Michael's Red Chicken

SERVES 4 | PREP 30 minutes | COOK 45 minutes

Ingredients

1 lemon, cut into 4 wedges

2 pounds fresh uncooked chicken tenders

Salt, to taste

Garam masala blend, to taste

2 tablespoons extra virgin olive oil

Sauce:

1 cup tomato sauce

1 cup heavy cream

1 tablespoon lemon juice

1 tablespoon fresh ginger, minced

2 teaspoons ground cumin

2 teaspoons chili powder

1 tablespoon fresh jalapeno pepper, minced

1 teaspoon garam masala blend

¼ teaspoon salt

¼ teaspoon cayenne pepper

¼ cup fresh cilantro leaves, chopped

Directions

Squeeze fresh lemon juice over the chicken tenders. Sprinkle with salt. Generously sprinkle the tenders on both sides with the garam masala seasoning.

Heat olive oil in a large skillet or Dutch oven. Brown the tenders on both sides. While they are browning, prepare the sauce.

In a medium bowl, mix the tomato sauce, cream, lemon juice, ginger, cumin, chili powder, jalapeno pepper, garam masala, salt, and cayenne pepper. Pour over the cooked chicken tenders in the skillet. Stir to coat the chicken. Reduce heat, cover, and simmer 30 minutes to blend flavors. Just before serving, sprinkle with the cilantro.

Notes

My son asks for this spicy chicken every time he comes home. I serve it with rice or pasta and a green salad.

Michael's White Chicken

SERVES 4 | PREP 30 minutes | COOK 40 minutes

Ingredients

2 pounds fresh uncooked chicken tenders

1 tablespoon dried Italian seasoning

1 tablespoon butter

1 tablespoon extra virgin olive oil

¼ cup dry sherry

2 garlic cloves, minced

1 cup heavy cream

½ cup half-and-half

¼ teaspoon nutmeg

½ cup Parmesan cheese, freshly grated

2 tablespoons fresh parsley, chopped

Salt and pepper, to taste

1 tablespoon lemon juice

Directions

Sprinkle the chicken tenders with Italian seasoning.

Heat the butter and olive oil in a large skillet. Brown the chicken on both sides. Remove the chicken and keep warm.

Add the sherry to the skillet and deglaze the pan, scraping up the drippings. Add the garlic and simmer over medium heat until the liquid is reduced by half. Add the heavy cream and half-and-half, lower the heat, and simmer until thickened. Stir in the nutmeg, Parmesan, parsley, salt, pepper, and lemon juice. Return the chicken to the pan with the sauce and simmer 15 minutes more.

Notes

My son designates his favorite foods by color. Both the red and white chicken are favorites. I serve both with rice or pasta and a green salad. His dessert of choice is OREO Cookie Freeze (page 248).

Bloomin' Onion Quiche with Goat Cheese and Thyme

SERVES 6 | PREP 25 minutes | COOK 45 minutes

Ingredients

1 refrigerated 9-inch pie crust

¾ cup leftover Outback Steakhouse Bloomin' Onion strips

1½ cups shredded cheese (I use goat cheese and mozzarella, but you can substitute your preferred shredded cheese)

3 eggs plus 2 egg yolks

1½ cups half-and-half

¼ teaspoon salt

⅛ teaspoon black pepper

1 teaspoon fresh thyme or ½ teaspoon dried thyme

Directions

Place the pie crust in 10-inch pie plate. To prevent a soggy crust, place a sheet of foil over the crust and weigh it down with pie weights. (It's worth the small investment, and you can buy them online. Or you can use dried beans.) Bake at 425 degrees for 8 minutes. Remove the weights and foil. Turn the oven down to 325 degrees.

Spread the Bloomin' Onion strips over the crust. Cover with the cheese.

In a medium-sized bowl, beat together the eggs, egg yolks, half-and-half, salt, pepper, and thyme. Pour over the onion strips and cheese. Bake at 325 degrees for about 45 minutes or until firm.

Notes

My son works with Bloomin' Brands, owner of Outback Steakhouse, home of the beloved Bloomin' Onion. I had the pleasure of creating one of these culinary delights in an Outback Steakhouse kitchen. Not one person knows the entire Bloomin' Onion recipe. It is in safe keeping, never to be shared. Several people know parts of it. The spicy seasoning mixture is secretly combined and sent to their restaurants around the world. I created this recipe to use leftover onions, if there ever are any.

Crispy Baked Parmesan Chicken

SERVES 8 | PREP 30 minutes | COOK 1 hour

Ingredients

½ cup butter

1 teaspoon garlic, minced

1 teaspoon Worcestershire sauce

1 teaspoon dry mustard

1 cup panko bread crumbs

½ cup grated Parmesan cheese

⅓ cup chopped fresh parsley

1 (3-ounce) can french fried onions, crushed.

4 chicken breasts, halved, boned, and skinned

Directions

Melt the butter in a large skillet and stir in the garlic, Worcestershire Sauce, and dry mustard. Set aside.

In a shallow dish combine the bread crumbs, Parmesan cheese, parsley, and french fried onions.

Dip each chicken breast half in the butter mixture and then in the bread crumb mixture. Place in a 9 x 13-inch baking dish. Drizzle any remaining butter mixture over the chicken.

Bake at 350 degrees until the chicken is tender, about 1 hour. My favorite way to bake it, if time permits, is to cover the dish with foil and bake at 300 degrees for 2 hours. Remove the foil during the last 30 minutes to let chicken brown. This makes the chicken even more moist and tender on the inside.

Notes

This is a favorite entrée from one of my first cookbooks. Both Elizabeth and Michael request it often. This delicious make-ahead dish is moist inside and crisp outside. I have revamped it a little from my original publishing.

Barbecued Meatloaf

SERVES 6 | PREP 20 minutes | COOK 1 hour 15 minutes

Ingredients

¾ cup soft bread crumbs

1 medium yellow or white onion, chopped

½ cup green bell pepper, chopped

1 beaten egg

½ (15-ounce) can tomato sauce

1 teaspoon salt

½ teaspoon black pepper

Dash garlic

Dash oregano

Dash Parmesan cheese

1 pound ground beef

Sauce:

Remaining ½ (15-ounce) can tomato sauce

⅓ cup water

2 tablespoons apple cider vinegar

2 tablespoons molasses

1 tablespoon yellow mustard

Directions

In a large bowl, stir together the bread crumbs, chopped onion, bell pepper, egg, and half of the tomato sauce. Add the salt, black pepper, garlic, oregano, and Parmesan. Add the ground beef and blend well. Shape into a loaf and put in baking dish.

Prepare the sauce by combining the remaining tomato sauce, water, vinegar, molasses, and mustard and mix well. Pour over the meatloaf.

Bake at 350 degrees for 1 hour and 15 minutes.

Notes

I love making this for my special friends, Ken and Donna Lewis. Few friends are as kind, caring, generous, and supportive as they. They have traveled the world eating in fancy restaurants, so they especially appreciated my down-home comfort food. Our faith and friendship make Donna and me as close as sisters. We talk most everyday even though we now live in different states.

Elizabeth's Creamy Gruyère Chicken

SERVES 8 to 10 | PREP 30 minutes | COOK 15 minutes (more if refrigerated earlier)

Ingredients

10 tablespoons butter, divided

1 cup mushrooms, sliced

2 tablespoons shallots, minced

½ cup dry sherry

2 pounds cooked chicken, shredded

4 tablespoons fresh basil, chopped

2 tablespoons fresh parsley, chopped

2½ cups whole milk

1½ cups heavy cream

2½ teaspoons salt

¼ teaspoon black pepper

¼ teaspoon cayenne pepper

¼ cup plus 2 tablespoons all-purpose flour

3 tablespoons Parmesan cheese, grated and divided

1¼ cups Gruyère cheese, shredded and divided

Brown rice

Fresh basil

Directions

Melt 2 tablespoons of the butter in a large skillet. Sauté the mushrooms and shallots until soft, about 5 minutes. Add the sherry and sauté for another 2 minutes. Remove to a large mixing bowl. Stir in the shredded chicken, basil, and parsley. Set aside.

In a medium saucepan, combine the milk, heavy cream, salt, black pepper, and cayenne pepper. Heat until very warm but not boiling. Set aside.

In a medium skillet, melt the remaining 8 tablespoons of butter and sprinkle in the flour to make a roux. Cook and stir constantly until golden brown. Add the roux to the milk mixture, whisking vigorously to prevent lumping. Bring to a boil while whisking to thicken. Cool for a few minutes and then stir in 2 tablespoons of the Parmesan and ¾ cup of the Gruyère cheese. Pour this cheese sauce over the chicken mixture.

Spread into a 9 x 13-inch baking dish. Sprinkle the Gruyère and Parmesan over the chicken.

Bake at 375 degrees until golden and bubbly. The time depends on whether it has been made ahead and refrigerated or frozen. Serve with brown rice garnished with fresh basil.

Notes

My daughter, Elizabeth, is an amazing natural cook. She does it with such ease. Everyone loves for her to prepare this dish for family, entertaining, or to take to a friend. My old cookbooks are filled with many variations for chicken in a creamy sauce. Along with the chicken, the main ingredient seemed to be creamy soup from a can. It's time that we make our own white sauce using natural cream and garden-fresh herbs. This recipe from Elizabeth has become one of my favorites, especially when *she* prepares it.

Slow-Cooked Barbecued Pork Tenderloin

SERVES 8 | PREP 10 minutes | COOK 7 hours

Ingredients

2 ½ pounds pork tenderloin

Barbecue basting sauce (your preferred brand)

Barbecue sauce (your preferred brand)

Directions

Place the tenderloins in your slow cooker and generously cover with the barbecue basting sauce. I use Stubb's Moppin' Sauce Bar-B-Q Baste. If you can't find anything specifically labeled "baste" or "basting sauce" in your grocery store, go for a thinner, vinegar-based barbecue sauce for this step and a thicker one for the last step.

Cover and cook on lowest setting for 6 or 7 hours.

Remove thoroughly cooked tenderloins from the cooker and drain away about two-thirds of the liquid. Shred the pork and place back in the cooker with the liquid. Generously cover with the barbecue sauce and slow cook another hour or so.

Notes

This is so easy that you don't really need a recipe and so good that you will want to make it often. My son and son-in-law both love it. The first night we have it with Black Bean Salsa (see recipe "Black Bean Salsa" on page 172) and corn bread. Then we enjoy the leftovers in tortilla wraps or on traditional sandwich buns with slaw.

Make-Ahead Sausage and Egg Casserole

SERVES 8 | PREP 25 minutes | COOK 30 minutes

Ingredients

1 pound bulk pork sausage

4 beaten eggs

2½ cups half-and-half

1 teaspoon dried sage

¾ teaspoon salt

¼ teaspoon black pepper

6 slices of bread (such as potato or brioche bread)

2 cups Cheddar cheese, grated

Directions

Brown and crumble the sausage. Drain well. Set aside.

In a mixing bowl, combine the eggs, half-and-half, sage, salt, and pepper. Place the bread in an 8 x 11-inch or 9 x 13-inch baking dish, covering the bottom. Spread the sausage over the bread. Pour the egg mixture over the sausage. Cover with the grated cheese.

This can be made ahead and refrigerated until ready to bake.

Bake at 350 degrees until cooked through, slightly puffed, and golden, which is about 30 minutes depending on whether or not it was refrigerated.

Notes

We never get tired of this sausage and egg combination. We serve it for every holiday brunch or when we have overnight guests. Our favorite brunch menu is this casserole, Holiday Rosemary Grapefruit (page 222) and Cheese Grits (page 240).

Fresh Shrimp Salad

SERVES 6 | PREP 30 minutes | COOK 2 minutes

Ingredients

1 lemon, quartered

1 tablespoon Old Bay Seasoning

1 tablespoon salt

2 pounds fresh shrimp, peeled and deveined

½ cup Vidalia onion, chopped

1½ cups celery, sliced

½ cup cucumber, chopped

1 cup mayonnaise

½ teaspoon Dijon-style mustard

1 tablespoon white wine vinegar

Salt and pepper, to taste

Lettuce

Fresh dill weed, minced

Directions

Fill a large pot with cold water and stir in the lemon quarters, Old Bay Seasoning, and 1 tablespoon of salt. Bring to a boil. Add the peeled, deveined shrimp and lower the heat to medium. Simmer until the shrimp are cooked, only about 2 minutes. Drain and chill until cold.

Cut the shrimp into bite-size pieces and place in a mixing bowl. Fold the onion, celery, and cucumber into the shrimp.

In another mixing bowl, combine the mayonnaise, mustard, and vinegar. Season with salt and pepper. Stir in the fresh dill (saving some to garnish).

Add enough of the mayonnaise mixture to the shrimp mixture to moisten generously. Chill until serving. Serve over lettuce and garnish with a sprinkle of fresh dill.

Notes

I serve this with Silver Queen corn on the cob—dressed with butter, salt, pepper, and minced fresh herbs—and ice-cold watermelon cut into wedges.

Roasted Brussels Sprouts

SERVES 4 | PREP 20 minutes | COOK 20 minutes

Ingredients

1 pound brussels sprouts

¼ cup extra virgin olive oil

1 tablespoon sesame oil

2 cloves garlic, minced

1 tablespoon fresh ginger, grated

2 tablespoons soy sauce

2 tablespoons rice vinegar

1 tablespoon honey

1 tablespoon mirin (optional)

½ teaspoon corn starch

⅓ cup green onions, sliced

⅓ cup dry roasted peanuts

Directions

Line a rimmed baking sheet with foil. Set oven to 400 degrees. Place the foil-lined baking sheet in the oven to heat while preparing the brussels sprouts.

Trim the ends of each brussels sprout and cut in half. Place in a bowl and toss with olive oil to coat. Spread evenly in one layer on the hot baking sheet. Return to oven and roast for approximately 20 minutes. Watch carefully and let brown but not burn.

While the brussels sprouts are roasting, prepare the sauce by heating the sesame oil in a small skillet. Sauté the garlic and ginger for 1 minute. Stir in the soy sauce, rice vinegar, honey, mirin, and cornstarch. Let the sauce simmer and thicken for about 1 to 2 minutes. Set aside.

Place the roasted brussels sprouts in on a serving platter. Toss to coat with sauce. Garnish with green onions and dry roasted peanuts.

Notes

This is a favorite weeknight meal served with Baked Salmon (page 181) and baked potato wedges.

Gingered Asparagus with Cashews

SERVES 6 | PREP 10 minutes | COOK 5 minutes

Ingredients

1½ pounds asparagus

2 tablespoons coconut oil

2 teaspoons sesame oil

1 tablespoon fresh ginger, finely chopped

1 tablespoon orange peel, freshly grated

1 tablespoon soy sauce

½ cup roasted cashews

Directions

Trim the tough lower stems off the asparagus and discard. Cut each stalk into 2-inch pieces.

Heat the oils in a large frying pan or wok. Stir-fry the asparagus and ginger until tender, about 5 minutes. Stir in the orange peel, soy sauce, and cashews. Serve immediately.

Notes

Broccoli Salad

SERVES 6 | PREP 20 minutes | COOK 10 minutes

Ingredients

4 cups fresh broccoli florets

½ cup red onion, thinly sliced

½ cup bacon, crisply cooked and crumbled

1 cup sweetened dried cranberries

½ cup mayonnaise

¼ cup sugar

1 tablespoon apple cider vinegar

Directions

Combine the broccoli, onion, bacon, and cranberries in a large bowl.

In a separate bowl, mix the mayonnaise, sugar, and vinegar. Pour over the broccoli and toss. Chill several hours.

Notes

Tomato Cheese Pie

SERVES 6 | PREP 30 minutes | COOK 30 minutes

Ingredients

Crust:

1¼ cups all-purpose flour

2 teaspoons Parmesan cheese, grated

½ teaspoon salt

1 teaspoon sugar

8 tablespoons (1 stick) cold butter, cut into pieces

⅓ cup cold whole milk (approximately)

Filling:

2 cups shredded Mexican cheese blend (divided)

⅔ cup mayonnaise

½ teaspoon garlic, minced

⅓ cup scallions, chopped

2 to 3 fresh tomatoes (depending on their diameter), sliced

¼ cup fresh basil, shredded

Directions

Crust:

Place the flour, Parmesan, salt, and sugar in a food processor. Mix lightly. Add the butter, pulsing until the mixture is crumbly. Add the milk gradually as needed while pulsing the processor until a soft dough is formed. Shape into a ball, cover with waxed paper, and refrigerate for about 15 minutes until it firms a little and handles well. On floured wax paper, roll the dough out into a 10-inch circle. Fit and trim into a 10-inch pie plate.

Filling:

Mix half of the shredded cheese with the mayonnaise, garlic, and scallions. Drain the tomatoes on paper towels if they are especially juicy. Spread the cheese mixture over the prepared pie crust. Cover the cheese mixture with tomato slices in a single layer. Sprinkle the basil over the tomatoes. Top with the remaining shredded cheese. Bake at 350 degrees for 30 minutes or until crust is browned. Cool for a few minutes before cutting into wedges.

Notes

Cheese Grits

SERVES 8 | PREP 30 minutes | COOK 1 hour

Ingredients

4 cups whole milk

1 cup quick-cooking grits (not instant)

8 tablespoons (1 stick) butter

½ teaspoon salt

¼ teaspoon cayenne pepper

2½ cups Cheddar cheese, grated

3 eggs, beaten well

Directions

Slowly bring the milk and grits to a boil in a large saucepan, being careful not to scorch the milk. Reduce heat and continue to stir until the mixture thickens, about 5 minutes. Remove from heat and stir in butter, salt, cayenne pepper, and cheese. Mix well. Whisk in the eggs. Pour into a well-greased 2½-quart casserole dish. Bake uncovered for 1 hour or until puffed and golden.

Notes

Elizabeth's Mac and Cheese

SERVES 8 | PREP 30 minutes | COOK 30 minutes

Ingredients

1 pound elbow macaroni or twists

8 tablespoons (1 stick) butter, divided

½ cup flour

2 teaspoons salt

¼ teaspoon black pepper

¼ teaspoon cayenne pepper

5½ cups whole milk

4½ cups white Cheddar cheese, grated and divided

2½ cups Gruyère cheese, grated and divided

6 slices of white bread, processed into crumbs

Directions

Cook and drain the pasta as directed on the bag or box.

In a large saucepan, melt 6 tablespoons of the butter. Stir in the flour, salt, and both peppers. Cook and stir constantly for 1 to 2 minutes. Gradually add the milk, stirring constantly. Cook and stir to make a smooth sauce. Stir in 3 cups of the Cheddar and ½ cup of the Gruyère until melted and smooth.

Stir the cooked pasta into the sauce and spread in a 9 x13-inch baking dish. Top with the remaining cheese.

Mix the remaining 2 tablespoons of butter with the fresh bread crumbs and sprinkle over the pasta and cheese.

Bake at 350 degrees for 30 minutes or until heated throughout, cheese is melted, and bread crumbs are browned.

Notes

I've made many different mac and cheese recipes, but no more. This is the one. It's the best. Elizabeth's version is now the family favorite.

Almond Joy Cake

SERVES 16 | PREP 30 minutes | COOK 25 minutes

Ingredients

½ cup slivered almonds

1 (15-ounce) box chocolate cake mix

1 (14-ounce) can sweetened condensed milk

1 (15-ounce) can cream of coconut

2 cups (1 pint) heavy cream

⅓ cup sugar, or to taste

1 cup shredded coconut (I like frozen best)

Directions

Toast slivered almonds for 7 minutes at 350 degrees and then set aside.

Prepare cake as directed on the packaging and bake as directed in a 9 x 13-inch baking pan.

Combine the sweetened condensed milk and cream of coconut. Punch holes in the baked cake with a toothpick and pour the mixture over the cake and allow to soak in.

When the cake cools, whip the cream with the sugar and spread over the cooled cake. Sprinkle with coconut and toasted almonds.

Notes

Almond Joy candy bars are a favorite of mine and my dear friend Marilyn's who did makeover segments on my noon show for years. Each time I would visit with her, I took candy bars for us. This cake is for her.

Marilyn is one of the most meaningful and memorable friends of my life. We worked together and traveled together. I can think of so many adventures with her and giggle just thinking about them, especially our snorkeling trip to Hawaii with Eric, another fun friend. Through all these decades, I can count on her to be there for the sad or the happy times, to cheer me up or cheer me on. She has taught me so many important life lessons. She is courageous, beautiful, loyal, brilliant, thoughtful, and kind She is also one of the funniest humans on this planet and can make me laugh like no one else.

Chocolate Chess Pie

SERVES 6 to 8 | PREP 20 minutes | COOK 35 to 40 minutes

Ingredients

1 unbaked 9-inch deep-dish pie crust

1½ cups sugar

3 tablespoons unsweetened cocoa powder

1½ tablespoons all-purpose flour

Dash salt

2 eggs, beaten

½ cup (1 stick) butter, melted

½ cup evaporated milk

1 teaspoon vanilla extract

Directions

Thaw or unroll the pie crust into a 9-inch deep-dish pie plate.

In a large bowl, mix together the sugar, cocoa, flour, and salt. Beat in the eggs, butter, milk, and vanilla. Pour the mixture into the pie crust.

Bake at 350 degrees for 30 minutes.

Reduce heat to 325 degrees and bake a little longer until filling seems almost firm. Do not overcook. It will cook a little more while cooling

Notes

This is a favorite recipe from my mom which I passed along to Elizabeth. For some inexplicable reason, my daughter makes it much better than I do. We all enjoy this quick and easy family recipe as often as possible!

Annette's Brownies

SERVES 16 | PREP 30 minutes | COOK 25 minutes

Ingredients

Brownies:

2 cups brown sugar

8 tablespoons (1 stick) butter

2 eggs

1 teaspoon vanilla extract

2 cups all-purpose flour

2 teaspoons baking powder

½ cup pecans, chopped (optional)

Frosting:

8 tablespoons (1 stick) butter

1 cup brown sugar

¼ cup whole milk

1 teaspoon vanilla extract

1½ cups confectioners' sugar, sifted

Directions

In a medium saucepan, melt the brown sugar and butter over medium low heat. Transfer to a mixing bowl and cool slightly.

In a separate bowl, beat the eggs with the vanilla extract. Temper the eggs by adding 1 teaspoon of the melted butter mixture to the eggs, then stir the tempered eggs into the slightly cooled butter mixture.

In a separate bowl, combine the flour and baking powder. Stir into the egg mixture in the mixing bowl. Add pecans to this batter if desired.

Grease and flour a 9 x 13-inch cake pan. Spread the batter into the prepared pan. Bake at 350 degrees for 25 minutes.

Prepare the frosting by melting the butter and brown sugar in a saucepan. Stir in the milk, vanilla extract, and cook the mixture for about 1 minute. Set aside to cool slightly.

Beat in the sifted confectioners' sugar.

Spread the frosting over the brownies.

Notes

Bertha was a very special lady. For a short time, she came to care for my children while I worked. She was very busy working for others, so she introduced me to her sister, Annette, who has had a major part in raising my children and caring for my home. She considers my children as hers too. I moved five times, and she has been a part of each move. We still stay in close touch. Every time we talk, she says, "If you ever need me any time of day or night, call me. I will always take care of you." She means that. No matter what. There are only a few people you know you can call in the middle of the night and they would come, no questions asked. Annette is one of those. What a blessing she is to me and my children. She and Bertha shared this delicious recipe with me.

DeDe's Messy Pie

SERVES 6 | PREP 30 minutes | COOK 30 minutes

Ingredients

Crust:

1¼ cups graham cracker crumbs

¼ cup sugar

5 tablespoons butter, melted

Filling:

1¼ cups sugar

3 tablespoons unsweetened cocoa powder

4 tablespoons cornstarch

3 cups whole milk

5 egg yolks (separated, save whites for meringue)

2 tablespoons butter

1 teaspoon vanilla extract

Meringue:

5 egg whites

¼ teaspoon cream of tartar

⅓ cup sugar

Directions

For the crust, combine the graham cracker crumbs, sugar, and butter. Mix well to moisten the crumbs. Press into a 10-inch pie plate. Bake at 400 degrees for 5 minutes.

For the filling, in a large saucepan or Dutch oven, combine the sugar, cocoa, and cornstarch. Stir to blend. In a large bowl or measuring cup, combine the milk and egg yolks, saving the whites in the bowl of an electric mixer. Pour the milk and egg mixture gradually into the dry mixture and mix well. Cook on medium heat stirring frequently until thickened. Stir in the butter and vanilla extract.

Pour the filling into the prepared crust. Cool slightly while making the meringue.

For the meringue, beat the egg whites until foamy. Add the cream of tartar, which stabilizes the egg whites, and beat until soft peaks form. Add the sugar and beat until thick and fluffy. Spread the meringue carefully over the pie filling. Bake at 400 degrees until browned. Cool at room temperature until the filling is set. (It will be too "runny" if cut while too hot.)

Notes

This was my favorite dessert growing up, and then it became my daughter's favorite dessert. Three generations now have loved it. It's worth making note that the custard for this is the same one my mom used for her amazing coconut cream pie and her banana pudding just by omitting the cocoa.

Why is it called Messy Pie? When my children, Elizabeth and Michael, were toddlers, they would watch their "DeDe" (my mom) make it, and when she would press the crust into the pie plate, they exclaimed, "MESSY pie!" The name stuck, and we even had a special pie plate made that said "DeDe's Messy Pie." Sadly, that pie plate is no longer with us, but the recipe and the memories remain. I hope it becomes a favorite at your house too.

OREO Cookie Freeze

SERVES 12 | PREP 30 minutes
COOK 10 minutes and freeze overnight

Ingredients

Crust:

24 OREO cookies (or other chocolate sandwich cookie), crushed in a food processor

4 tablespoons sugar

⅓ cup butter, melted

Filling:

½ gallon vanilla or coffee ice cream, softened

Topping:

1 cup sugar

1 (5-ounce) can evaporated milk

4 (1-ounce) squares semisweet chocolate

6 tablespoons butter

1 teaspoon vanilla extract

Optional Garnishes:

Whipped cream, toasted pecans, maraschino cherries, or toasted pecans

Directions

For the crust, combine the cookie crumbs, sugar, and melted butter. Mix well and press into 9 x 13-inch pan. Freeze until firm (about 1 hour).

For the filling, spread the softened ice cream over the frozen crust. Freeze until firm.

For the topping, combine the sugar, evaporated milk, chocolate squares, and butter in a saucepan. Melt together and simmer for 1 minute. Remove from heat and stir in vanilla extract. Let cool until lukewarm. Pour over the ice cream layer and freeze at least 4 hours.

Garnish as desired.

Notes

For over two decades, this dessert has been one of the most requested, especially by my son, Michael, who now lives in Tampa. I have it ready and waiting whenever he comes home. It's perfect for guests because it must be made ahead of time.

Perfect Pecan Pie

SERVES 6 | PREP 15 minutes | COOK 50 minutes

Ingredients

1 (9-inch) refrigerated pie crust

4 eggs

1 cup light corn syrup

¾ cup sugar

⅓ cup butter, melted

Pinch salt

1 cup pecans, chopped

¾ cup pecan halves

Directions

Unroll the pie crust into a 9-inch pie plate.

Beat the eggs with corn syrup, sugar, melted butter, and salt.

Stir in the chopped pecans and pour into prepared crust. Arrange pecan halves on top.

Bake at 350 degrees for 50 minutes.

Notes

I make this pie for my friend Bryan McRae every Thanksgiving because it is his favorite. I've known and loved him since he was a server in a restaurant over two decades ago. Now he is an artist, and his business Botanica has gone global. His beautifully preserved botanicals are in gorgeous homes around the world. His friendship never wavers. He designed the flowers for everything from my daughter's wedding to my mother's funeral. His gorgeous work is seen throughout my home and my daughter's. Just to let you know the kind of friend he is, he promises that if I should ever become incapacitated, he will do my hair and makeup as long as necessary. I must make sure I always live near Bryan.

Pink Things

SERVES 14 | PREP 20 minutes

Ingredients

½ gallon vanilla ice cream, softened

1 small (10-ounce) jar maraschino cherries (without stems), drained and chopped

1 cup pecan pieces

1 bag (approximately 12 ounces) coconut macaroon cookies, crushed

1/3 cup dry sherry (optional)

Directions

Combine the ice cream, cherries, pecans, crushed cookies, and sherry in a large bowl until well mixed. Pour the mixture into muffin tins lined with cupcake wrappers. Freeze. Serve frozen.

Notes

This recipe is from Emily Gardner, the mom of Jane, my best friend growing up. She kept these delightful little desserts in her freezer. I'm guessing they had a more formal name, but Jane and I made a beeline for the "pink things" in her freezer every visit.

Jane and I have such an extraordinary friendship. We have been best friends since we were in preschool dance around the age of four. We grew up together and have always been inseparable. We went to elementary, junior high, and high school together. Then we were roommates at UNC Chapel Hill. We *married* roommates from UNC Chapel Hill. Our daughters were roommates at Chapel Hill and also continue to be the best of friends. Though we live in different cities, we text or talk several times a week and can still finish each other's sentences. She continues to "look out for me" as she has done my whole life, and she never fails to make me laugh.

My Favorite Rum Cake

SERVES 8 to 12 | PREP 30 minutes | COOK 45 minutes

Ingredients

Rum Cake:

½ cup pecans, chopped

1 box yellow cake mix

1 (3.4-ounce) box vanilla instant pudding

½ cup dark rum

½ cup water

½ cup vegetable oil

4 eggs

Hot Rum Glaze:

1 cup sugar

½ cup (1 stick) butter

¼ cup dark rum

¼ cup water

Directions

Grease and flour 1 large or 2 small tube pans. Sprinkle the chopped pecans over the bottom of the greased pan(s) and set aside.

Combine the cake mix, pudding mix, ½ cup rum, water, oil, and eggs in the bowl of an electric mixer. Beat for 2 minutes on medium speed. Pour into the prepared pans. Bake at 325 degrees for approximately 45 to 50 minutes or until done. It will take a little less time in the smaller pans.

While the cake is baking, prepare the hot rum glaze. Combine the sugar, butter, rum, and water in a small saucepan. Boil gently for 2 minutes. Remove from heat to cool slightly.

When the cake is done and still in the cake pan(s), prick the warm cake with a toothpick many times to make small holes. Pour the prepared warm rum glaze over the hot cake. Allow to cool in the pan for about 15 to 20 minutes. Turn out onto a cake platter.

Notes

This has become a favorite holiday gift from my kitchen, according to my friends. I make sure that Laura Vinroot Poole has one for her family and one for her store every Christmas. She styles me in her amazing curated collection from Capitol, and I make cakes. Perfect! This works well in one large Bundt pan or two smaller ones. Sometimes a smaller cake is preferred.

Special Day Dessert

SERVES 10 | PREP 20 minutes

Ingredients

2 cups heavy cream

1 (8-ounce) package cream cheese, softened

1 cup powdered sugar

1 teaspoon vanilla extract

1 (8-ounce) can crushed pineapple, well drained

2 packages lady fingers, split

Fresh seasonal fruit or canned pie filling of your choice

Directions

In a large bowl, whip the cream until soft peaks form and set aside.

In another large bowl, beat together the cream cheese, powdered sugar, and vanilla. Fold the pineapple and whipped cream into the cream cheese mixture.

Line a springform pan with the split lady fingers. Pour in the cream filling. Chill several hours.

Cover with fresh fruit or canned pie filling.

Notes

This is another recipe from my first cookbook that has stood the test of time. It is memorable, not only because it's delicious, easy, presents beautifully, and everyone seems to want the recipe, but also for an additional unforgettable reason.

I appeared on a *live* nationally syndicated television show airing all over the country. I featured this favorite of mine. The dessert is prepared in a springform pan, which means at serving time, you remove the sides of the pan and place the metal bottom holding this lovely dessert on your serving platter. I used a crystal pedestal cake stand. When I picked up the pedestal part and whirled around to show "my masterpiece" to the camera, the entire dessert flew off the platter and flopped onto the floor in a huge gloppy mess. (Seeing the ingredients, you can guess what it looked like.) Throughout the rest of the show, the producers kept returning to the shot of what I had prepared ... especially for them ... piled up on the floor.

Television keeps you humble.

Troutman Pound Cake and Teddy Bears

SERVES 20 | PREP 1 hour | COOK 1 hour and 15 minutes

Ingredients

Cake:

½ cup (1 stick) butter, softened

1 cup vegetable shortening

3 cups sugar

5 eggs

3 cups cake flour

½ teaspoon salt

2 teaspoons vanilla extract

1 cup whole milk

Teddy Bear Sauce (optional):

½ cup (1 stick) butter

2 cups sugar

½ cup evaporated milk

1 teaspoon vanilla extract

2 cups salted peanuts, chopped

Directions

For the cake, beat the butter, shortening, and sugar together until smooth and creamy. Add eggs one at a time, beating well. In a separate bowl, combine the flour and salt. Alternate adding small portions of the flour mixture and the milk to the creamy mixture. Beat in the vanilla.

Pour into a tube pan and bake at 325 degrees for 1 hour and 15 minutes.

To turn this traditional pound cake into Teddy Bears, bake instead in a 9 x 13-inch cake pan at 325 degrees for 1 hour. Let cool completely.

Prepare the Teddy Bear dipping sauce by combining the butter, sugar, and milk in a saucepan. Cook until bubbly, about 2 to 3 minutes. Stir in the vanilla extract.

Cut the sheet cake into squares and dip into the Teddy Bear sauce. Then dip into the salted peanuts.

Notes

I wrote about my always-delightful friend Curtis earlier in the book. Leave it to him to come up with this clever and delicious dessert from his house with the pink oven in Troutman, North Carolina.

Smoothies

SERVES 1 | PREP 5 minutes

Ingredients

Mango Banana Smoothie

1 banana

½ cup frozen mango pieces

⅓ cup vanilla yogurt

½ cup orange-mango juice blend

Chocolate Peanut Butter Protein Shake

1 cup whole milk

3 ice cubes

1 banana

2 tablespoons peanut butter

1 small scoop vanilla ice cream

3 tablespoons chocolate protein powder (your preference on protein type)

Blueberry Vanilla Smoothie

1 cup milk

3 ice cubes

1 cup frozen blueberries

1 tablespoon almond butter

3 tablespoons vanilla protein powder (your preference on protein type)

Directions

For the Mango Smoothie, combine the banana, mango, yogurt, and juice in a blender and blend until smooth.

For the Chocolate Peanut Butter Protein Shake, combine the milk, ice, banana, peanut butter, and protein powder in a blender and blend until smooth.

For the Blueberry Vanilla Smoothie, combine the milk, ice, blueberries, almond butter, and protein powder in a blender and blend until smooth.

Notes

I became an expert at making smoothies after my accident when I had to drink all my food for three months. Right after my surgery, when I looked very scary, my precious friend, Kim Pleasants, and her sister, Pam, came to my home and made gallons of juices for me. I can always count on Kim to cry with, pray with, or laugh hysterically with. She will leave a message on my phone that will keep me giggling for days. Everyone needs a Kim in life. These smoothies made me realize how blessed I am, even during difficult times.

Ultimate Cheesecake

SERVES 12 | PREP 30 minutes | COOK 1 hour

Ingredients

Crust:

1½ cups graham cracker crumbs

3 tablespoons brown sugar

1 teaspoon cinnamon

½ cup (1 stick) butter, melted

Filling:

3 (8-ounce) packages cream cheese, softened

1½ cups sugar

4 eggs

2 cups sour cream

2 tablespoons lemon juice

½ teaspoon vanilla extract

1 cup heavy cream

Directions

For the crust, combine graham cracker crumbs, brown sugar, cinnamon, and butter. Press into a 9-inch springform pan. Refrigerate while preparing the filling.

For the filling, beat the cream cheese until smooth. Gradually add the sugar, beating until fluffy. Add eggs one at a time, beating to mix well. Add the sour cream, lemon juice, vanilla extract, and heavy cream and mix 1 minute. Pour into the prepared crust.

Wrap the bottom of the springform pan with several sheets of foil in a crisscross pattern. Place the pan in a larger pan and fill the larger pan with water halfway up its sides. This water bath will keep the cheesecake from cracking as it bakes. Place in the oven and bake at 325 degrees for 1 hour. (Don't open the door during cooking.) After 1 hour, turn off the oven and leave another hour without opening the door. Refrigerate several hours before serving.

Notes

This is a simple, classic cheesecake, but to me, it is simply the best. Because of my cooking shows and cookbooks, I've made hundreds of miscellaneous cheesecakes. This one, from my dear friend Linda Hodges many years ago, remains my all-time favorite. While it is rich and creamy, it somehow seems lighter than many cheesecakes. You can get creative with most any topping, from a chocolate sauce to fresh seasonal berries and whipped cream.

Rita's Baked Apple Pie Shake

SERVES 1 | PREP 10 minutes

Ingredients

1 small apple (your preferred type)

¼ teaspoon cinnamon

Pinch nutmeg

2 tablespoons water

¼ cup vanilla protein powder (your preference on protein type)

1 cup unsweetened almond milk

⅓ cup full fat coconut milk

1 teaspoon pure vanilla extract

1 tablespoon ground flax seed, optional

1 tablespoon chia seeds, optional

Ice, optional

Directions

Slice the apple, remove seeds, and place in microwave-safe bowl. Sprinkle with cinnamon and nutmeg. Add water and cook for about 3 minutes on high.

Combine the apples, water, protein powder, almond milk, coconut milk, vanilla extract, and (if desired) flax and chia seeds in a blender and blend until smooth and creamy.

Sprinkle with additional cinnamon and nutmeg.

Optionally, blend in a handful of ice cubes.

Notes

This healthy recipe comes from Rita Pearson, niece of Denzel and Pauletta Washington and a wellness expert. She does her best to keep me healthy. She shared this yummy recipe and reminded me it is food for life. Rita and I have celebrated our faith and friendship for many years now even though she is in Beverly Hills and I'm in Charlotte. She is another dear friend who saw me through my crazy health-crisis year with such love, encouragement, care, and thoughtfulness. She always makes me smile and feel special, although she is really the special one.

About the Author

Her many years of television, radio, and magazines have made Barbara McKay one of Charlotte's most popular and recognizable media personalities.

For her numerous TV shows and specials, Barbara has traveled the world to interview top newsmakers, major stars in the entertainment industry, and prominent sports figures. After hosting her daily top-rated show *Top O' the Day* for twenty-three years on CBS affiliate WBTV, Barbara went on to create, executive produce, and host several other lifestyle shows locally, regionally, and nationally.

A wide range of brands and companies have leveraged Barbara's position as a trusted advisor to her viewers, readers, and social media followers. Recognized for her professionalism and communication expertise, she has served as a spokesperson for national and international companies.

Additional highlights in Barbara's media career include roles in CBS daytime dramas *The Guiding Light* and *As the World Turns*, as well as appearances as a lifestyle reporter on nationally televised features.

In addition to success in broadcast media, Barbara has also launched and published two successful magazines in the Charlotte market: *Barbara McKay's Premier Bride* and *Barbara McKay's Simply the Best.*

Thanks to her community activism and philanthropy, Barbara was presented the Maya Angelou Women Who Lead Award for her contributions and commitment to higher education and for her personal and professional achievements.

Barbara shares her personal passions—food, fashion, family, and furry friends—on the digital landscape. She provides a fun and fabulous outlet for trendsetters, animal lovers, and foodies on her website BarbaraMcKay.com She can be found on Instagram @simplybarbaramckay.

Thank you, Duke Mansion

I chose The Duke Mansion as the setting for my book cover because this beautiful, historical landmark has been the location of some of my most favorite times in Charlotte, from visiting when it was a private residence to attending many special occasions, including my daughter's wedding rehearsal dinner. The four acres of gorgeous gardens, the exquisitely appointed rooms, and the wonderful staff all symbolize the grace, elegance, and hospitality of the South, the place that has been my life-long home.

Barbara McKay
Coming Home
Recipes and Reflections
from a Life in the Spotlight